WortCunning

A folk Medicine Herbal

WORTCUNNING
A Folk Medicine Herbal

TROY BOOKS

First North American Edition, 2020
Second Printing, 2020
ISBN 978-0-7387-6590-7

Originally published by Troy Books Inc. 2018
ISBN 978-1-909602-33-5

Llewellyn Publications is a registered trademark of Llewellyn Worldwide Ltd.

Cataloging-in-Publication Programme data is on file with the British National Bibliography.

Llewellyn Worldwide Ltd. does not participate in, endorse, or have any authority or responsibility concerning private business transactions between our authors and the public.

All mail addressed to the author is forwarded but the publisher cannot, unless specifically instructed by the author, give out an address or phone number.

Any Internet references contained in this work are current at publication time, but the publisher cannot guarantee that a specific location will continue to be maintained. Please refer to the publisher's website for links to authors' websites and other sources.

Llewellyn Publications
A Division of Llewellyn Worldwide Ltd. 2143 Wooddale Drive
Woodbury, MN 55125-2989 www.llewellyn.com

Printed in the United States of America

Acknowledgements

I would like to thank Gemma and Jane at Troy Books for their continued support and encouragement of my work – it means a great deal. And, inevitably, my thanks and gratitude go to my husband Anthony, who has to live with the vagaries of an eccentric writer, two dogs, run his own business and get my dinner on time!

Dedication

None of this would ever have happened without the kind input of an unknown group of people nearly forty years ago. So, to the family group of Crafters who gave me the base material for this book, I would like to dedicate this work to you. I hope I've done you proud.

Contents

INTRODUCTION
A Folk Medicine Herbal

In the early 1980's, I was working with a small coven in a town on the coast of Suffolk, East Anglia. One of the members mentioned that she was in touch with a family group of witches, in Sussex I think (or in that area). She had been corresponding with them for a while and had gained their friendship. They were offering her some of their family recipes on herbal medicine and, with their permission, would I be interested in seeing them and taking a copy too? I said "Yes, I would be very interested" and so, sometime later, she presented me with the information that they had sent. It was a set of the old-fashioned card-index cards, complete within the box. There was a brief note at the beginning, describing where, and how, the plants grew and could be found, followed by the rest of the cards in alphabetical order, both ailments and the herbs to treat them.

I dutifully copied them all down into one of my work books and there they stayed, almost unused, for the next thirty five-odd years. I looked at the notes from time to time and even tried out some of the remedies, which seemed to work well. However, my main interests lay in different areas at that time and so I really made little use of them. It was only when I finally took my own qualifications in herbal medicine and had a greater knowledge of the subject that I looked at them in any real detail. By then, I had lost touch with both the originators of the material and the coven member that had lent me the originals, so I was unable to check any details, or my memory, of what I was told at the time.

As I recall, some of the cards had been typed, the rest were hand-written and were in more than one hand; I think there were at least three different persons writing. This would seem to be borne out by the different descriptive styles used on the cards, the language used and the forms of notation. From subsequent study, some of the herbs used are not the usual ones that would normally be taken for the given ailments; some herbs that are standard in herbal

medicine are not used at all and there are quite a few that rarely come up in a medical herbal anyway. This all leads me to think that this is the collected lore of a family, or group of people, writing down the recipes they were using that were outside of an orthodox training system. How old any of this is and how far back the recipes/lore goes, I have now no way of knowing or finding out but, from the internal evidence, it looks to be at least three generations. This would take the information back to near the beginning of the twentieth century, if not earlier.

I was never asked to keep this material secret nor, as far as I am aware, was it ever intended to be so. There is certainly nothing in the material that could be considered "oath-bound" or *sub-rosa*. Therefore, I have decided to publish this material in its entirety, for two reasons. Firstly, in my work as a herbalist and magical practitioner, I am often asked if I know of a genuine, folk or traditional, herbal that could be used. Usually I have to say 'no', as I know of nothing else like this in print. I now think that this material should be available to those who would find it useful and be able to work with it. Secondly, purely in the

interests of preserving and disseminating this information to a wider audience of those who would find it interesting.

The first section, the "Habitat Code", is the brief note at the beginning of the cards, describing where the plants grow, etc. as previously mentioned, with the letter keys then being applied to the herbs themselves. The main herbal which follows is exactly as I transcribed it, including some of the idiosyncratic spellings of the Latin names of the plants. These are not always the correct names, or the names that the individual herbs are now classified under but I wanted to reproduce the material in the exact form I received it. (I also wanted to show that this herbal is probably not the product of orthodox training but a genuine folk tradition). In the section on the magical use of the herbs, at the back of this book, I have amended the Latin names to what I consider to be the correct classifications – any errors are, therefore, my own. I should also just note that the measurements given are British Imperial measurements and care should be taken when converting them to other systems; measurements in any form of medical

treatment are important and should be adhered to as given.

On that point, I should just say that neither I, nor the publishers, can take any responsibility for any results obtained in using this material, by the reader. Whilst I have used some of the recipes myself to good effect and I know from my own training and experience that the information given here should cause no harm, any plant-based therapy may cause unknown effects on any given individual. It is always wise to do your own research first and seek qualified medical advice before using any of these remedies. Having said this, it is my hope that these remedies will be used and form a valid part of the readers' natural healing therapy.

Nigel G. Pearson.
Suffolk, England.
Midsummer 2018.

HABITAT CODE

If one considers that the first line (horizontal), of letters in the code is that which specifies the wet or dryness of the land type on which the given plant may be found, and that "A" means that the ground is water and that "E" means the ground is dry (Desert dry), then one see's soon enough that "B", "C" and "D" must be variables between the point. They are. To make this all clearer, I shall list now the number of the line, give its meaning (i.e. what aspect of the soil type/habitat it describes) and a precise meaning to each variant.

Top line;
A = Water.
B = Wet.
C = Damp.
D = Moist.
E = Dry.

Second line down;
A = Very Acid.

B = Mild Acid.
C = Neutral.
D = Mild Calcareous.
E = Very Calcareous.

Third line down;
A = Very Fertile.
B = Fertile.
C = Medium.
D = Poor.
E = Very Poor.

Bottom line;
A = Dense Woods.
B = Woods.
C = Open Woods.
D = Scrub.
E = Open.

So, from the above then, we may deduce that a plant which is coded as e.g.
E.
A.
E.
D.E
would be a plant that prefers very dry, very acidic, very poor soils, in the open or on the edge of woods. Such a plant may be termed

as a heath loving plant, as that is where the plant is most liable to find such conditions.

Let us look at another example;
C.D.
D.E.
B.C.
A.B.
Now, here we have a plant which we may look for on damp or moist, calcareous and moderately fertile soils, in a deep or very deep shade. A limestone wood should provide the ideal situation for such a plant.

WORTCUNNING
A Folk Medicine Herbal

❧A❧

Aconite (*Aconitum napellus*)
May – Sept. Saturn.
Poisonous plant. Do not touch.
1) B.C. D
2) B.C.D.E.
3) A.B.C.
4) A.B.C.D.

Aches & Pains (See: **St. Johnswort***, **Mallow***).

Agrimony (*Agrimonia eupatoria*)
June – August. Jupiter.
<u>Coughs & Diahorrhea</u>; *1oz of herb, infused in 1pt of water. Take ½ cup.*
<u>Liver disorders</u>; *Mix; Agrimony @ 3 parts, Boldo Leaves @ 3 parts, Alder Buckthorn @ 2 parts, Calamus root @ 2 parts. Boil 1 tablespoon of the mix in 1 pint water for 10 mins. Take one cup before and after meals. Meals should be light for 48 hrs.*

1) D.E.
2) C.D.E.
3) B.C.D.
4) E.

Alder (*Alnus glutinosa*)
Venus.
<u>Sore throat</u>; *Take a pinch of powdered bark in ½ cup water and gargle.*
<u>Tonic</u>; *2 leaves infused in ½ cup water.*
<u>Foot wash</u>; *Use a cooled infusion of a handful of herbs to 2 pints water.*
1) B.C.
2) B.C.D.
3) A.B.C.
4) B.C.D.E.

Alder Buckthorn (*Frangula alnus*)
May – June.
<u>Constipation</u>; *Mix Alder Buckthorn bark @ 4 parts, Ash leaves @ 2 parts, Alder flowers @ 2 parts, Mint @ 2 parts. Infuse 2 teaspoons in a cup of water; drink one or two cups before bedtime.*
1) B.C.D.
2) A.B.C.
3) C.D.
4) A.B.C.D.E.

Anaemia (See: **Nettles**).

Angelica (*Angelica sylvestrus*)
July – Sept. Sun.
<u>Cystitis</u>; *Infuse 1 teaspoon of seeds in a cup of boiling water for 10/15 mins. Let stand till cool, strain and take 2 cups per day.*
<u>Blood purifier</u>; *Infuse 1oz of dried and cut root in 1 pint water for 30 mins. (Keep the pot covered). Take 2 tablespoons 4 times a day.*
<u>Apertive</u>; *Mix Angelica @ 2 parts, Yarrow @ 3 parts, Centaury @ 10 parts, Marjoram @ 4 parts. Infuse 1 teaspoon for 10 mins. In a covered cup. Take 1 hr. before meals.*
1) B.C.
2) B.C.D.
3) A.B.C.
4) A.B.C.D.E.

Antiseptic (See: **Garlic**, **Balm**, **Thyme**).

Apertive (See: **Angelica**).

Arthritis (See: **Ash**, **Birch**).

Asafoetida (*Ferula foetida*)
Saturn.
<u>Epilepsy/Hysteria/Colic</u>; *A small pinch rolled*

inside a Balm leaf and swallowed whole.

Ash (*Fraxinus excelsior*)
May – Sept. Saturn.
<u>Laxative/Arthritis/Gout</u>; *1oz leaves infused in 1 pint water. Take ½ cup.*
1) C.D.E.
2) B.C.D.E.
3) D.E.
4) A.B.C.D.E.

❧ B ❧

Balm/Lemon Balm (*Melissa officionalis*)
July – Sept. Jupiter.
<u>Fever/Headaches/Painful Periods</u>; *1oz herb infused in 1 pint water. Take ½ cup.*
<u>Antiseptic</u>; *Make a poultice of Balm in a muslin cloth. Infuse for 10/15 mins. And apply to wound. You may re-soak the poultice a few times in its own juices. Use about ½ pt. water to prepare a poultice for an average-sized "septic-finger" type of wound.*

Basil (*Ocimum basilicum*).
July – Sept. Mars.
<u>Nervous headache</u>; *Infuse 1 teaspoon in a cup, covered for 10/15 mins. Strain, sweeten and sip hot. Take up to 2 cups per day.*

Beech (*Fagus sylvatica*)
Saturn.
<u>Diahorrhea</u>; *Chew fresh leaves.*
<u>Wounds</u>; *Use fresh Beech water or a fresh leaf poultice.*
1) C.D.E.
2) A.B.C.D.E
3) B.C.D.E.
4) A.B.C.D.E.

Bergamot (*Monarda didyma*)
June – Sept. Mercury.
<u>Nausea</u>; Infuse 1 teaspoon in a covered cup for 15 mins.

Bilberry (*Vaccinium myrtillus*)
June – Aug.
<u>Diabetes</u>; *(To aid in treatment). Boil 2 handfuls each of Bilberry & Nettle leaves in 4 pts. water for 20 mins. Allow to stand till cool. Strain and take 2 pts. in a day.*
<u>Diahorrhea</u>; *(In Men). Soak a handful of Bilberry leaves for 24 hrs. in a bottle of Bordeaux wine. Take a glass with and between each meal. (Follow diet as under* **Tormentil***).*
1) D.E.
2) A.B.
3) C.D.E.

4) B.C.D.E.
Blocked Up Nose (See: **Mullein**).

Blood Purifiers (See: **Burnet, Angelica**).

Birch (Silver) (*Betula alba*)
April – May. Venus.
<u>Arthritis</u>; *(A) Mix: Birch leaves @ 3 parts, Meadowsweet @ 2 parts, Couch Grass root @ 2 parts, Marjoram @ 2 parts, Coltsfoot @ 1 part.*

(B) Mix: Willow Bark @ 3 parts, Elder @ 2 parts, Golden Rod @ 2 parts, Rosemary @ 2 parts.

Alternate the use of the above two mixes with the use of that given under Ash, each 3 days. i.e. use a different mix each third day. To prepare the above; add 2 table spoons of one mix to 3 pts. of boiling water. Keep water heated for a few minutes, cover and allow to stand off the heat for 10 mins. Strain and drink warm.
<u>Local applications</u>, (See **Linseed**).
Supplement the diet with; Garlic, Asparagus, Celery, Fennel, Onions, Tomatoes and Fruit.
<u>Mouth Wash</u>; *1 oz. leaves infused in 1 pt. of water. Use ½ cup.*
<u>Skin Diseases</u>; *Apply distilled Bark Oil.*
1) C.D.E.
2) A.B.C.D.E.

3) D.E.
4) C.D.E.

Boneset (*Eupatorium perfoliatum*)
Influenza; *1 oz. infused in 1 pint of water. Take one warm wine glass full every half hour, for two hours. The patient should stay in bed.*
Tonic; *1 tsp. infused for 30 mins in a cup of water. Take 1 tsp. (cold), 3-6 times per day.*

Borage (*Borago officionalis*)
May – Sept. Jupiter.
Tonic/Depression/Mouthwash; *Steep or infuse 1 oz. of fresh flowers in wine or water OR 1 oz. of dried herb infused in 1 pint water for 15 mins.*
Chest Cold/Kidney Complaints; *Infuse the herb as above. To be taken by the wine glass dosage.*

Breathing Troubles (See: **Coltsfoot, Garlic**).

Bronchitis (See: **Elecampane, Horehound, Liquorice Root** (**Spanish**), **Comfrey**).

Broom (*Cytisus scoparius*)
High Blood Pressure; *Infuse 1 oz. of stem tops in 1 pint water. Take ½ cup.*
1) D.E.

2) A.B.C.
3) C.D.E.
4) D.E.

Bruises (See: **Shepherds Purse**).

Burns (See: **Lady's Mantle**).

Burdock (*Arctium lappa*)
July – Sept. Venus.
Rheumatics/Chest Diseases/Skin Diseases/
Haemorrhoids. *Decote 1 oz. dried root in 1 ½
pints water. Take ½ cup or apply externally.*
1) D.E.
2) B.C.D.
3) B.C.D.
4) D.E.

Burnet (*Pimpinella saxifraga*)
May – Sept.
Blood Purifier; *Infuse 1 tsp of herb in a covered
cup of water. Only one cup per day.*
Wounds; *(Astringent); one handful of herbs
decocted in 1 pint of water for 15 mins. Keep
it covered and let it cool before applying it on a
bandage.*
1) E.
2) C.D.E.

3) D.E.
4) C.D.E.

✢C✣

Carrot (*Daucus carrota*)
Mercury.
<u>Flatulence</u>; *1 oz. of leaves infused in 1 pint of water. Take ½ a cup.*
<u>Eye Conditions</u>; *Eat grated root, raw.*
1) D.E.
2) C.D.E.
3) B.C.
4) E.

Catnip (*Nepeta cataria*)
June - Sept. Venus.
<u>Nausea</u>; *Infuse 1 tsp. in a covered cup for 15 mins. Strain and drink cool. Up to two cups per day.*
<u>Sedative</u>; *Infuse 1 oz. in 1 pint (covered) water. Take; Adults – 2 tablespoons full, Children – 2/3 teaspoons full. Cool.*
<u>Tonic</u>; *Mix; Catnip @ 2 pts, Motherwort @ 1 pt, Skullcap @ 2 pts, Sage @ 1 pt, Chamomile @ 2 pts. Infuse, covered, for 10 mins. Strain and sweeten. Take cool. Take 1 wine glass, 3 times a day and before bed.*
ALWAYS TAKE THIS HERB COOL.

1) D.E.
2) C.D.
3) A.B.C.
4) E.

Centaury (*Centaurium erythrae*)
June – Sept. Sun.
<u>Stomach Cramps</u>; (See: **Marjoram**).
<u>Sluggish Gall Bladder</u>; *Mix; Centaury@ 2 pts, Mugwort @ 2 pts, Mint @ 2 pts, Liquorice @ 3 pts, Rosemary @ 10 pts. Infuse 1 tsp of mix in a covered cup for 15 mins. Strain and sip slowly. Diet: avoid fatty foods, eggs, pastry. Eat: toast, vegetables, fruit. Grill all meat.*
1) C.D.E.
2) A.B.C.D.E.
3) C.D.E.
4) C.D.E.

Chamomile (*Anthemis nobilis*)
June – Sept.   Sun.
<u>Tonic/Nerves</u>; *1 oz. of flowers or herb taken infused in 1 pint water. 1 cup to be taken. Infuse, covered, for 15 mins.*
<u>Toothache</u>; Apply to the tooth.
<u>Indigestion</u>; *Mix; Chamomile @ 2 pts, Lemon Balm @ 2 pts, Mint @ 3 pts, Yarrow @ 3 pts. Put a tsp of the mix into a cup, cover and infuse*

for 10 mins. Sweeten and take a cup full after every meal or as often as required.
1) D.E.
2) B.C.
3) D.E.
4) E.

Chestnut (Sweet) (*Castania sativa*)
Jupiter.
<u>Whooping Cough/Cough/Fever</u>; *1 oz. leaves infused in 1 pint of water. Take 1 tablespoon.*

Chickweed (*Stellaria media*)
April – June.   Moon.
<u>Skin Ulcers/Kidney Diseases/Scurvy</u>; *Whole plant eaten raw, for internal purposes. Made into a poultice or ointment for external.*
1) B.C.D.E.
2) B.C.D.E.
3) A.B.C.D.E.
4) B.C.D.E.

Chillblanes
<u>Complete course of treatment as follows</u>;
CIRCULATION STIMULATION; *mix equal parts of Angelica, Alpine Lady's Mantle, Golden Rod, Hawthorn Flowers, Yarrow. Prepare the foregoing fresh each morning thus; Infuse 4*

*tablespoons of the mix in 2 pints of water. Take
by the cup full every day.*

Part Two.
*Each night, before bed, bathe affected parts in this;
Hawthorn, Shepherds Purse 3 pts, Sanicle, Kidney
Vetch 1 pt. Infuse 5 tablespoons in 4 pints. Stand
for 10 mins. Add cold water till bearably hot.
After bathing, cover hand/foot with a lukewarm
compress of mix 3. Wrap in canvas and cover with
woollen sock/glove.*

Part Three (Compress)
*Mix equal parts of; Blessed Thistle, Mallow
Leaves, Walnut Leaves, Sage, Coltsfoot leaves.
Infuse 3 tablespoons in 2 pints of water for 15
mins or till lukewarm. Complement diet with
Carrots, Parsley, Tomatoes, Blackcurrant juice
and Lemon juice.*

Cinquefoil (*Potentilla reptans*)
May – Sept. Jupiter.
Diarrhoea; Infuse 1 oz. in 1 pint of water.
Take one wine glass full – cool.
Cuts and Abrasions; (Astringent); Infuse 1
tsp. in a cup and wash the wound with this.
1) C.D.E.
2) A.B.C.D.

3) A.B.C.
4) D.E.

Colds (See: **Elder, Garlic, Hazel, Rowan; Borage, Marshmallow, Meadowsweet, Mullein** (Blocked Nose), **Peppermint, Violet***).

Colic (See; **Asafoetida**).

Coltsfoot (*Tussilago fafara*)
Feb – April. Venus.
Dry Coughs/Breathlessness; 1 oz. of leaves decocted in 2 pints of water for ½ hour. Can be smoked.
1) C.D.E.
2) B.C.D.E.
3) B.C.D.E.
4) E.

Comfrey (*Symphytum officionale*)
May – June. Saturn.
<u>Bronchitis</u>; *Infuse 1 tsp. in a cup of water for 15 mins.*
<u>Diahorrhea</u>; *Decote ½ oz. of dried, ground root in 1 quart of water or milk for 15-20 mins. Take by the wine glass as often as needed.*
<u>N.B.</u> *Comfrey is an excellent herb. It is, 9/10 times,*

beneficial to add 1 teaspoon of the dried herb to most of the remedies given for "everyday" maladies.
1) B.C.
2) B.C.D.
3) A.B.C.
4) C.D.E.

Constipation (See: **Ash, Alder, Buckthorn***).

Couch Grass (Witch Grass)
March/April – Sept./Oct. Jupiter.
Cystitis; *Mix; Couch Grass @ 1 pt, Ground Barley @ 1 pt Comfrey @ ½ pt. Infuse in a covered cup of water for 15 mins. Take ½ at once and ½ later. Take as little salt as possible. Dress warmly.*

Coughs (See: **Agrimony, Chestnut, Coltsfoot, Elecampane, Garlic, Horehound, Liquorice Root** (Spanish), **Mandrake** (White Bryony), **Nettles, Poppy** (Opium), **Turnip, Marshmallow, Thyme**).

Cowslip (*Primula veris*)
April – May Venus.
Influenza; *Mix; Cowslip flowers @ 2 pts, Lime flowers @ 2 pts, Meadowsweet @ 3 pts Violet*

@ *3 pts. Infuse 2 tablespoons in 1 pint of water. Cover and allow to infuse for 10/15 mins. Strain, sweeten and drink. Stay in bed. Wrapping the feet in bandages soaked in warm, vinagered water may also help.*

X. E.

X. A.B.C.D.E.

X. E.

C.D.E.

Cuts and Abrasions; (See Wounds) (See: **Burnet** (Astringent), **Beech**, **Cinquefoil**, **Plantain**, **Thyme**).

D

Dandelion (*Taraxacum officionale*)

April – June   Jupiter.

<u>Tension/High Blood Pressure/Kidney Troubles</u>; *1 oz. of root, leaf or flower infused in 1 pint of water. Take 1 cup.*

<u>Nausea</u>; *Infuse 2 tsps. of cut and dried root in a cup of water for 30 mins. Take one or two cups per day.*

1) B.C.D.

2) A.B.C.D.E.

3) A.B.C.D.E.

4) C.D.E.

Deadly Nightshade (*Atropa belladonna*)
June – Sept. Saturn.
Poisonous Plant. Do Not Touch.
1) D.
2) C.D.E.
3) B.C.
4) C.D.E.

Depression (See: **Borage**, **Dittany of Crete**, **Feverfew** (Melancholia), **Foxglove**)

Diabetes (See: **Bilberry**).

Diarrhoea (See: **Agrimony, Beech, Hazel, Comfrey, Plantain, Tormentil**).

Dittany of Crete
Venus.
Tonic/Depression/Wounds; *1 oz. infused in 1 pint of water. ½ cup taken. Use for a poultice.*

Dock (*Rumex obtusifolias*)
Jupiter.
Nettle Stings/Itching/Freckles; *1 oz. infused in 1 pint of water, applied externally. Bruised, fresh leaves may be applied.*
1) C.D.E.

2) B.C.D.
3) A.B.
4) D.E.

❧ E ❧

Elder (*Sambucus nigra*)
May – Sept.   Venus.
<u>Colds/Epilepsy</u>; *Infuse 1 oz. of bark or flowers in 1 pint of water. Take ½ cup. Can also be fermented into tonic wine (use flowers or berries).*
1) C.D.E.
2) B.C.D.E.
3) A.B.C.D.
4) C.D.E.

Elecampane (*Inula helenium*)
June – Sept. Mercury.
<u>Tonic/Coughs/Bronchitis</u>; *Infuse 1 oz. dried root in 1 pint of water. Take ½ cup.*

Elm (*Ulmus*)
Saturn.
<u>Wounds/Gout</u>; *Ground bark mixed with brine. Use as a poultice.*
1) B.C.D.
2) B.C.D.

3) B.C.D.
4) E.

Epilepsy (See:**Asafoetida, Elder, Sage**).

Eye Conditions (See:**Carrot, Eyebright***)

Eyebright (*Euphrasia nemorosa*)
June – Oct. Sun.
<u>Eye Disorders</u>; *Infuse ¼ tsp. in a cup of water. Apply to the eye, cold.*
OR
Mix equal parts of Eyebright, Crushed Fennel, Centaury, Sanicle & Speedwell. Infuse one teaspoon in a cup for ten mins. Allow to cool and make a compress from the liquor.
<u>Poor Memory</u>; *Take an infusion of one teaspoon to one cup of water – and don't forget!*
1) D.E.
2) A.B.C.D.E.
3) D.E.
4) D.E.

❧ F ❧

Fennel (*Foeniculum officionale*)
July – Sept. Mercury.
<u>Nausea</u>; *Mix equal parts of Fennel, Mint, Balm, Chamomile & Centaury. Infuse 1 tablespoon in 1*

pint of water for 5 mins. Sip as cooling.
<u>Flatulence</u>; *Mix; Fennel @ 3 pts, Coriander @ 3 pts, Caraway @ 2 pts, Yarrow @ 2 pts. Infuse 1 tsp. of mix in a covered cup for 10 mins. Take after every meal.*
1) D.E.
2) B.C.D.
3) A.B.C.
4) E.

Feverfew (*Chrysanthenum parthenium*)
June – Sept. Venus.
<u>Afterbirth Fever/Migraine/Melancholia</u>;
Infuse 1 oz. in a pint of water and take ½ a cup. Not to be taken during pregnancy. Sedative: Infuse 1 oz. of dried flowers in 1 pint of water. Cover and allow to stand till cool. Strain, sweeten and take ½ tea- cup doses as needed.
<u>Colds</u>: *Prepare as above, but take hot.*
<u>Tonic Tea</u>; *As for Melancholia.*

Fever (See: **Balm, Chestnut**)

'Flu (See: **Boneset, Cowslip***)

Flatulence (See: Carrot, **Pennyroyal, Peppermint, Fennel**)
Foxglove (*Digitalis pupurea*)

June – Sept. Venus.
Poisonous plant, do not touch.*
*N.B. Extract (Digitalis) used in heart complaints.
1) D.
2) A.B.
3) C.D.E.
4) C.D.E.

❧ G ❧

Gall Bladder (sluggish) (See: Centaury)

Garlic (*Allium sativum*)
June – Aug. Mars.
<u>Antiseptic</u>; *Use juice in a poultice.*
<u>Colds/Coughs/Asthma</u>; *Mix Garlic juice with honey or sugar. Use equal parts. Take one teaspoonful or one capsule.*

Gentian (*Gentiana amerella*)
Mars.
Dull Headache; Decote ½ oz. of finely cut root in ½ pint of water for 15 mins. Take two tsps. It may be sweetened with honey and/or Peppermint, Balm or Lime Blossoms may be added to advantage.

Gout (See: Ash, Elm.

H

Hawthorn (*Crataegus oxycantha*)
Mars.
<u>Heart Disease</u>; *1 oz. powdered berries in 1 pint of Scotch. Take one teaspoon 4 times a day.*
<u>Hypertension</u>; *Make up the following two mixes;*

A) Hawthorn Leaves @ 3 pts, Horsetail @ 3pts, Olive Leaves @ 2 pts, Orange Flowers @ 2 pts.

B) Lavendar Flowers @ 3 pts, Shepherds Purse @ 3 pts, Alpine Lady's Mantle @ 2 pts, Mistletoe @ 2 pts. Infuse 1 tsp in a covered cup for 5 mins. Take a cup of mix A on Monday & Tuesday and take mix B for the rest of the week. Eat plenty of Garlic, Onion, Parsley and Veg/Fruit. Avoid alcohol and tobacco.
1) C.D.E.
2) B.C.D.E.
3) A.B.C.D.E.
4) C.D.E.

Hazel (*Coryllus avellana*)
Mercury.
<u>Colds/Diahorrhea</u>; *Take several nuts, crushed, in milk or mead.*
<u>Heavy Periods</u>; *Ground up shells in red wine.*

1) C.D.
2) B.C.D.
3) A.B.
4) A.B.C.D.E.

Headache
Nervous; (See: **Rosemary, Basil**)
Throbbing; (See: **Mellilot**)
Dull; (See: **Gentian**)
Across the Forehead; (See: **Peppermint**)
Due to Flatulence; (See: **Peppermint**)
Top of the Head; (See: **St. Johnswort**)
General; (See: **Balm, Thyme**)
Migraine; (See: **Feverfew**)

Heartsease (*Viola tricolour*)
March – Aug. Venus.
Acne: Mix; *Heartsease @ 3 pts, Alder Buckthorn bark @ 3 pts, Birch Leaves @ 2 pts, Meadowsweet @ 2 pts. Add one tablespoon to 1 pint water (boiling). Allow to stand till cool before straining. Take 1-2 cups in the afternoon and evening. Also, supplement meals with salads containing Radish, Dandelion, Water Cress. Dress warmly.*
1) C.D.E.
2) B.C.D.E.
3) A.B.C.D.
4) D.E.

Hemlock (*Conium maculatum*)
June – Aug. Saturn.
Poisonous plant, do not touch.
1) C.D.
2) B.C.D.
3) A.B.C.
4) E.

Hemlock Water Dropwort (*Oenanthe crocata*)
June – Aug.
Poisonous plant, do not touch.
1) B.
2) B.C.D.
3) A.B.C.D.
4) E.

Henbane (*Hyoscyamus niger*)
May – Sept. Saturn.
Poisonous plant, do not touch.
1) D.
2) B.C.
3) A.B.C.

Herb Robert (*Geranium robertianum*)
May – Aug.
<u>Ulcers</u>; *(Mouth Wash); Mix; Herb R. @ 5 pts,*
Sage @ 3 pts, Thyme @ 2 pts. Infuse 1 tsp. in a

cup for 15 mins. Also, rinse the mouth often with ½ glass of water containing 20 drops of tincture of Myrrh and a little salt. Supplement the diet with acidic fruit, peeled apples, lemon juice. Avoid sweet foods.

1) C.D.
2) A.B.C.D.E.
3) A.B.C.
4) A.B.C.D.

High Blood Pressure (See: Broom, Dandelion)

Holly (*Ilex aquafolium*)
May – June Saturn.
Rheumatism; *(Women), Mix; Holly Leaves @ 2 pts, Meadowsweet @ 2 pts, Birch Leaves @ 2 pts, Chestnut Leaves @ 2 pts, Cinnamon Bark @ 1 pt, Plantain Leaves @ 1 pt. Decote 2 tablespoons of the mix in a pint of water for 15 mins. Strain, sweeten and take one cup, every half hour in the morning.*

1) D.E.
2) A.B.C.D.E.
3) D.E.
4) A.B.C.D.E.

Hops (*Humulus lupulus*)
July – Sept. Mars.

<u>Tonic/Worms/Jaundice</u>; *1 oz. of Hop heads infused in 1 pint of water. Take one cup.*
<u>Insomnia</u>; *For insomnia, a pillow filled with Hop flowers may be slept on to ease the complaint.*
<u>Nerve Tonic</u>; Mix; *Hops @ 2 pts, Horsetail @ 2 pts, Anise (ground) @ 2 pts, Mint @ 3 pts, Chamomile @ 1 pt. Infuse two tablespoons of mix in 1 pint of water. Cover and stand for 15 mins. Take a cup before meals and/or in the evening.*
1) A.B.C.
2) C.D.
3) A.B.
4) A.B.C.D.E.

Horehound, White (*Marrubium vulgare*)
June – Sept Mercury.
<u>Coughs/Bronchitis/Tonic</u>; *1 oz. of herb per 1 pint of water. Infuse for 15 mins. Take ½ cup.*

Black Horehound (*Ballota nigra*), *will expel worms. 1 teaspoon of herb infused in 1 pint of water for 15 mins.*
1) D.E.
2) B.C.D
3) A.B.
4) E.

Hypertension (See: **Hawthorn leaves**)

Hyssop (*Hyssopus officianalus*)
July – Sept Jupiter.
<u>Bruises</u>; *crush the fresh plant and apply it to the affected part.*

Hysteria (See: **Asafoetida**, Rue, **Tansy**, **Feverfew** (sedative), **Catnip** (sedative), **Skullcap** (sedative))

🦁 I 🦁

Indigestion (See; Flatulence. Chamomile,
Sage (acidic),
Marjoram (stomach cramps).

Insomnia (See; **Hops, Poppy, Valerian**)

🦁 J 🦁

Jaundice (See; **Hops, Sage**)

Juniper (*Juniperis comunis*)
May – June Jupiter.
<u>Kidney diseases</u>; *1oz of berries infused in 1pint of water for 15 mins. Take one cup every/ per 2 hrs.*
<u>Rheumatism (Men)</u>; *Mix; Juniper @ 2pts,*

Ash @ 2pts, Lime @ 2pts, Parsley root @ 2pts, Coltsfoot @ 1pt, Thyme @ 1pt. Infuse two tablespoons of the mix in 1 pint of water. Allow to stand till cool. Take one cup every ½ hour in the morning.

1) D.E.
2) A.B.E.
3) D.E.
4) D.E.

K

Kidney Ailments (See; **Chickweed, Dandelion, Juniper, Borage, Couch, Grass***)

L

Lactation (See; **Vervain**)

Lady's Mantle (*Alchemilla vulgaris*)
May – Sept. Venus.
<u>Burns</u>; *Mix; Lady's Mantle @ 4pts, Plantain Leaves @ 2pts, Sanicle @ 2pts, Marigold Flowers @ 2pts. Infuse 5 tablespoons of mix in 2 pints of water until cooled. Strain off and use the water to wash the burn.*
Larkspur (*Consolida ambigua*)

June – Aug.
Poisonous plant. Do not touch.

Lavendar (*Lavandula officinalis*)
July – Sept. Mercury.
<u>Nervous Exhaustion</u>; *Bruise up some dried herb and infuse it for 15 mins in a covered cup. Take one cup per day.*

OR

<u>In the morning</u>; *Mix; Lavendar @ 1pt, Chamomile @ 1pt, Liquorice @ 2pts, Mint @ 3pts, Valerian @ 3pts. Infuse 2 tsps in a cup. Cover and allow to stand for 5 mins. Drink slowly.* (See Hops).

Linseed
<u>Arthritis</u>; *For local applications (external), make a poultice of Linseed flour to which should be added a handful of freshly ground Fenugreek seeds.*

Liquorice Root Spanish. (*Glycyrhieglabra*)
Mercury.
<u>Coughs & Bronchitis</u>; *Mix equal parts of; Liquorice root, Coltsfoot flowers, Mallow flowers, Thyme, Aniseeds (ground). Infuse 2 tablespoons in 1pint water, keep covered for 10 mins. Take no more than 3 cups per day. Eat plenty of fruit, especially citrus.*

Liver Disorders (See; **Agrimony**)

Loosestrife, Yellow (*Lysimachea vulgaria*)
Venus.
<u>Stops Bleeding</u>; *1oz per pint of water. Take ½ a cup.*
<u>Sore Throats;</u> *As above; Gargle.*

Lovage (*Levisticum officinale*)
June – Aug   Sun.
<u>Menstruation; (To aid)</u>; *Infuse 1oz of dried herb in 1 pint of water for 15 mins. Keep covered.*

🌿M🌸

Mallow (Common/Tree/Marsh)
<u>Aches & Pains</u>; *Mix: Mallow leaves @ 6pts, Chamomile @ 4pts. Infuse 2 handfuls of the mix in 2 pints of water. Strain and add cold water until the bath is comfortably hot. Bath your feet and/or hands in it. Eat little and often. Try to get plenty of currants, almonds and black currant juice.*
(Wound pains; see:- Marsh Mallow)

Common	Marsh
1) D.E.	1) B.C.

2) B.C.D.E.   2) C.D.
3) A.B.C.   3) B.C.
4) E.   4) E.

Marigold (*Calandula officionalis*)
May – Oct. Sun.

Cuts; *Make a wash to bath minor cuts and abrasions thus; Infuse 1oz of dried flowers and leaves in 1 pint of water for 15 mins. Wasp Stings; Rub the affected part with fresh Marigold flowers.*

Marjoram (*Origanum marjorana*)
July – Sept. Mercury.

Nausea; *An infusion known as "Spring Tea" is famed for the treatment of an upset stomach; Infuse one teaspoon of leaves and tops in a covered cup for 15 mins. Take up to two cups per day.*

Stomach Cramps; *Mix; Marjoram @ 4pts. Yarrow @ 3pts. Angelica @ 2 pts. Centaury @ 1 pt. Infuse one tea spoon of the mix in a covered cup for 10 mins.*

1) D.E.
2) D.E.
3) D.E.
4) C.D.E.

Marsh Mallow (*Althaea officionalis*)
Aug – Sept. Venus.

Coughs/Colds/Nausea; *Infuse 1oz in a pint of*

water for 10-15 mins. Take like tea. To reduce pain while a wound is healing; Mix; Mallow leaves @ 3 pts. Comfrey @ 2 pts. Plantain @ 2 pts. Sage @ 2pts. Arnica @ 1 pt. Infuse 3 tablespoons of mix in 2 pints of water. Stand for 15 mins. Avoid sugar and sweet foods.

1) B.C.
2) C. D.
3) B.C.
4) E.

Meadowsweet (*Spiraea ulmaria*)
June – Sept. Jupiter.
Cold Recovery; Infuse one teaspoon of herb in a covered cup for 15 mins. Take one cup after meals.
1) B.C.
2) B.C.D.E.
3) A.B.C.
4) C.D.E.

Mellilot, Ribbed (*Melilotus officionalis*)
June – Sept.
Throbbing Headache; *Infuse ¾ oz of herb in a pint of water and stand for 15 mins. Take a cooled wine glass full 3 or 4 times a day.*
1) C.D.E
2) B.C.D.
3) A.B.

4) E.

Motherwort (*Leonorus cardiaca*)
July – Sept. Venus.
<u>Tonic/Stimulant</u>; *Infuse one teaspoon for 15 mins in a cup of water. Take one cup per day. This is a powerful tasting herb; it is advisable to add Lavendar to taste.*
1) D.
2) B.C.
3) A.B.C.
4) E.

Mouth Wash (See; (**Silver**) **Birch, Borage, Herb Robert*** (**Ulcers**).

Mugwort (*Artemisia vulgaris*)
July – Sept. Venus.
To promote Menstruation; 1 oz infused in 1 pint of water. Take ½ a cup.
1) D.
2) B.C.
3) A.B.C.D.
4) C.D.E.

Mullein (*Verbascum thapsus*)
June – Sept.   Saturn.
<u>Blocked up Nose/Fuggy Head</u>; *Boil ½ oz*

herb in a kettle and inhale the steam. Add a few poplar buds (Balm of Gilead).
1) D.
2) B.C.D.
3) B.C.D.
4) C.D.E.

❧N❧

Nausea (See; **Bergamot, Catnip, Dandelion, Marjoram, Pennyroyal, Spearmint, Fennel***)

Nervous, Disorders (See; **Chamomile, Dandelion** (Tension). **Rosemary** (Nerve Tonic). ***Lavendar** (nervous Exhaustion). **Peppermint** (Sedative). ***Hops,** ***Wild Strawberries**.

Nettle Rash (See; **Dock**)

Nettle (Stinging) (*Urtica dioica*)
June – Sept. Mars.
<u>Coughs/Tonic/Poison Antidote</u>; *1 oz of leaves or seeds, decoted in 1 pint water. Take ½ cup.*
<u>Anaemia</u>; *Mix; Nettle leaves @ 4pts. Birch leaves @ 2pts. Walnut leaves @ 2pts. Sage leaves @ 2pts. Infuse 1 teaspoon of mix in a cup for 15 mins. Take one cup between meals. Eat plenty of*

Carrots and Spinach.
1) B.C.D.
2) B.C.D.
3) A.
4) A.B.C.D.E.

Night Sweating (See; **Wild Strawberries**)

❧P❧

Parsley (*Petroselinum sativum*)
June – Sept. Mercury.
Menstruation (to promote)/Kidney Stones;
*1 oz infused 10/15 mins in 1 pint of water. Take
½ a cup.*

Peppermint (*Mentha piperita*)
July – Sept. Venus.
Headache, Across the Head and/or Due to
Flatulence; *Infuse 1 teaspoon of herb in a cup for
5 mins. Take one or two twice daily after meals.*
Cold; *At the first sign of a cold, mix equal
amounts of; Peppermint, Elder flowers, Yarrow.
Infuse 1 teaspoon in a covered cup for 15 mins.
Take hot.*
Sedative; *Mix equal parts of; Peppermint, Wood
Betony, Caraway Seeds. Treat as above for cold.
Drink before bed.*

<u>Flatulence</u>; *As for Headache. (Above)*.

Pennyroyal (*Mentha polegium*)
July – Oct. Venus.
<u>Flatulence/Nausea</u>; *Infuse 1 teaspoon of herb in a cup for 15 mins. Keep covered and drink warm.*

Periods
<u>Painful</u>; (See; **Balm, Wormwood**)
<u>Promotion of</u>; **Feverfew, Mugwort, Parsley, Rue, Sage, Lovage, Southern Wood**.
<u>Stem Heavy</u>; **Hazel**.
<u>Tonic</u>; **Rosemary**.

Plantain (*Plantago major*)
June – Oct. Venus.
<u>Diarrhoea</u>; *Infuse 1 oz of leaves in a warm place for 20 mins. Strain it and let it cool. Take 1-2 wine glasses, 3-4 times a day.*
<u>Cuts & Abrasions</u>; *Crunch up fresh leaves and apply.*
1) D.
2) B.C.D.E.
3) A.B.C.D.
4) E.
Poppy, Red (*Papaver rhoeas*)
June – Oct. Moon.
<u>Insomnia/Coughs/Pain Killer</u>; *Boil a green*

seed in 1 pint milk, with sugar. Take ½ cup.
1) D.E.
2) B.C.D.
3) A.B.
4) E.

Privet (*Ligustrum vulgare*)
May – June Moon.
<u>Freckles/Sore Throat</u>; *1 oz of flowers or leaves in fused for 10 mins in 1 pint of water. Wash with it or gargle.*

❦R❦

Rheumatism (See; *****Holly** (Women). *****Juniper** (Men).

Rosemary (*Rosmarinus officionalis*)
March – April Sun.
<u>Nervous Headache</u>; *Infuse 1 teaspoon of herb in a cup for 10 mins. Take a small cup full. Cool.*
<u>Tonic/Bad Stomach/Nerve Tonic</u>; *Infuse 1 oz of herb in a pint of water for 15 mins. Take 1 cup.*
<u>Menstrual Tonic</u>; *Mix equal parts of; Rosemary, Sage, Chamomile, Shepherds Purse, Mugwort. Infuse 3 tablespoons in 2 pints of water. Take a cup full, hot, every ½ hr.*

Rue (*Ruta graveolans*)
June – Sept. Sun.
<u>Periods (Promote)/Hysteria</u>; *Infuse 1 oz of the herb in 1 pint of water. Take ½ a cup.*

❧S❧

Sage (*Salvis officionalis*)
June – Aug. Jupiter.
<u>Menstruation (promotion)/Jaundice/Epilepsy</u>; *1 oz per pint of water. Infuse 15 mins. Take ½ cup.*
<u>Sore throat</u>; *Infuse 2 teaspoons in a cup for 15 mins. Strain. Sweeten and take. Improvement may be expected immediately.*
<u>Indigestion (Acidic)</u>; *Mix; Sage @ 3 pts. Liquorice @ 3 pts. Coriander @ 2pts. Wormwood @ 2 pts. Infuse 1 teaspoon in a cup for 10 mins. Sip, 1 hour before meals.*

Sanicle (*Sanicula europaea*)
May – July.
<u>Used in the treatment of burns</u>; *to aid a wound in healing, mix equal parts of; Sanicle, Sage, St. Johnswort, Plantain, Marigold. Infuse 3 tablespoons in 2 pints of water for 10 mins. Allow to cool, then re-heat until luke-warm. Use as luke-*

warm compress and/or bath.
1) D.E.
2) C.D.E.
3) A.B.
4) A.B.C.

Savory (*Satureia hortensis*)
July – Sept. Mercury.
Stomach Cramps; *Infuse 1 teaspoon in a covered cup for 10 mins. Take one cup of WARM sweetened mix as often as is needed.*

Scurvy (See; **Chickweed**)

Sedatives (See; **Hysteria**)

Shepherds Purse (*Capsella buesa-pastoris*)
Dec. - Jan.
Bruises; *Mix; Shepherds Purse @ 3 pts. Lady's Mantle @ 3 pts. Silverweed @ 2 pts. Woodruff @ 2 pts. Infuse 1 tablespoon in 1 pint of water, cover and stand for 10 mins. Take one or two cupfuls between meals. Eat as little sweet food as possible.*
1) C.D.E.
2) A.B.C.D.E.
3) A.B.C.D.E.
4) E.

Skin Ailments (See; **(Silver) Birch, Burdock, Chickweed** (Ulcers) **Dock** (Freckles or Itching))

Skullcap (*Scutalaria galericulater*)
June – Sept.
<u>Sedative Tea</u>; *Powder the herb and infuse a teaspoon in a covered cup for 10/15 mins. Take up to two cups per day in ½ cup doses.*
<u>Nervous Headache</u>; *Mix one part each of Skullcap, Peppermint, Sage. Prepare as above and take a warm cupful as often as needed.*
1) A.B.C.
2) A.B.C.D.E.
3) A.B.C.D.
4) B.C.D.E.

Sore Throat (See; **Sage, Alder, Thyme**)

Southernwood (*Artemisia abrotanum*)
July – Oct. Venus.
<u>Menstruation</u>; *(To promote); Infuse 1 oz. of herb in a pint of water. Cover for ten minutes, then strain and sweeten to taste.*
Not to be used in pregnancy.

Spearmint (*Mentha viridus*)

July – Oct. Venus.

<u>Nausea</u>; *Mix equal amounts of; Spearmint, Fennel, Dill, Anise, Chamomile, Catnip. Infuse 1 teaspoon in a covered cup for 15 mins. Sip slowly.*

OR

Mix equal parts of Spearmint, Chamomile, Catnip, Valerian. Prepare as above, drink warm every 2 hours.

<u>Spearmint Tea</u>; *Infuse 1 teaspoon of herb in a covered cup for 10 mins. Drink sweetened, warm or chilled.*

Spots (Acne) (See; Heartsease)

Stimulant (See; Motherwort)

St. John's Wort (*Hypericum – Various*)

July – Sept. Sun.

<u>Headache on Top of the Head</u>; *Infuse 1 teaspoon in a cup for 10 mins. Take 2 tablespoons 3 times a day or as needed.*

<u>Aches & Pains</u>; *Mix equal parts of; St. John's Wort, Hawthorn Leaves, Lavendar Leaves, Balm Leaves, Elder Flowers. Infuse 1 teaspoon in a cup for 10 mins. Take between meals.*

(See; **Mallow**)

1) C.D.E.

2) A.B.C.D.E.

3) C.D.E.
4) C.D.E.

T

Tansy (*Tanacetum vulgare*)
July – Oct. Venus.
Worms/Tonic/Hysteria; *Infuse 1 oz. In one pint of water. Take one cup.*
Freckles; *Crush and apply to the affected skin.*
1) D.
2) B.C.D.
3) B.C.D.
4) D.E.

Thorn Apple (*Datura stramonium*)
July – Oct. Jupiter.
Poisonous plant. Do not touch.
1) D.
2) B.C.D.
3) A.B.C.D.
4) E.

Thyme (*Thymus vulgaris*)
June – Sept. Venus.
Worms/Indigestion/Bad Stomach/Promotes Labour; *Infuse 1 oz. of herb per 1 pint of water. Take ½ cup frequently.*

<u>Headache/Sore Throat/Cough</u>; *Infuse 1 teaspoon and a pinch of Rosemary in a covered cup for 10 mins. Take as needed.*

Tonics (See; **Alder**, **Borage**, **Catnip**, **Chamomile**, **Dittany of Crete**, **Elcampane**, **Feverfew**, **Hops**, **Horehound**, Nettle, **Rosemary**, **Tansy**)

Toothache (See; **Chamomile**)

Tormentil (*Potentilla erecta*)
May – Sept. Sun.
<u>Diarrhoea</u>; *mix; Tormentil root @ 3 pts. Plantain @ 3 pts. Purple Loosestrife Flowers @ 2 pts. Thyme @ 2 pts. Infuse 2 tablespoons of mix in 1 pint of water. Cover and allow to stand. Take one cup with and between each meal. (Men see Bilberries). Avoid greasy food, eat only well cooked meat. Fruit and veg; Carrots, Artichokes, Sprouts, Black Currants, Lemons and Bilberries. Chew all food well.*
1) C.D.E.
2) A.B.
3) B.C.D.E.
4) E.

🌿U🌿

Urinary Tract Infections (See; **Angelica**

(cystitis) **Couch Grass** (cystitis))

❧V❧

Valerian (*Valeriana officionalis*)
June – Aug. Mercury.
<u>Insomnia</u>; *Infuse 1 teaspoon of dried ground root, in a pint of water for 10 mins. (covered). Take 1 cup before going to bed.*
OR
IF NEEDED MORE REGULARLY; MIX;
Valerian @ 2 pts. Anise @ 2 pts. Marjoram @ 2 pts. Balm @ 2 pts. Infuse a tablespoon in 2 pints of water for 10 mins. Drink a cup in the early morning.
1) B.C.D.
2) C.D.E.
3) A.B.C.D.E.
4) A.B.C.D.E.

Violet (*Viola rivianiana*)
March – May/July – Sept. Venus.
<u>Colds</u>; *Mix equal parts of; Violet flowers, Elder, Meadowsweet, Liquorice, Holly. Infuse 2 tablespoons in 1 pint of water for 10 mins. Strain off and take one cup every hour, in the morning.*

OR

Concoct and use the following inhalation; Mix; Mint @ 3 pts. Thyme @ 3 pts. Origano @ 2 pts. Hay (Flr heads) @ 2 pts. Put 2 tablespoons in 2 pints of boiling water. Inhale fumes. Keep warm and dry, drink blackcurrant juice, grapefruit and lemon juice. Eat radishes.

1) D.
2) A.B.C.D.E.
3) C.D.E.
4) A.B.C.D.

Vervain (*Verbena officionalis*)

June – Oct. Venus.

<u>Lactation (to promote)</u>; *Mix equal parts of; Vervain, Nettle, Basil, Anise, Fennel (ground). Infuse 2 tablespoons in 1 pint of water. Keep covered, leave for 5 mins. Take 1 cup every 2 hours. Also, eat lots of veg, especially carrots. Eat dates. Drink milky coffee and chicoree. Drink weak beer at night.*

1) D.E.
2) B.C.D.E.
3) B.C.D.E.
4) E.

🌿W🌸

Wasp Stings (See; **Marigold**)

Wild Strawberry (*Frangania vesca*)
April – July.

<u>Nervous Exhaustion/Night Sweating</u>; *Mix;*
W/S berry leaves @ 2 pts. Nettle leaves @ 2 pts.
Walnut leaves @3 pts. Sage @ 3 pts. Infuse 1 teaspoon
in a cup of water for 10 mins. Take 1 cup after meals.
1) C.D.E.
2) B.C.D.E.
3) A.B.C.
4) C.D.E.

Witch Hazel (*Hamamelus virginiana*)

<u>Night Sweating/Nervous Exhaustion</u>; *Mix*
equal parts of; Witch Hazel leaves, Oak Bark,
Tormentil Root, Eucalyptus leaves, Walnut leaves.
Decote 5 tablespoons in 4 pints of water for 5
mins. Strain off and add 1 / 2 pints of water.
Bath feet or hands in this solution.

Woodruff (*Asperula odonata*)
April – June. Mars.

<u>Cuts and bruises</u>; *Apply crushed, fresh leaves to*
the wound.

<u>Periods (Tonic for, and mild preventative of)</u>;
<u>Mix</u>; *Woodruff @ 2 pts. Tormentil @ 2 pts. Silver*
Weed @ 2 pts. Lady's Mantle @ 3 pts. Cinnamon
@ 1 pt. Simmer 3 tablespoons of the mix in 2 pints

of water for 5 mins. Take a cup full every ½ hour.
1) C.D.E.
2) B.C.D.E.
3) A.B.C.
4) A.B.C.

Worms (See; **Hops, Horehound, Tansy, Thyme, Wormwood**)

Wormwood (*Artemisia absinthium*)
Aug. - Sept. Mars.
<u>Worms Tonic</u>; *1 oz. per pint of water. Infuse for 10 mins and take ½ cup. Period Pains; Steep 1 teaspoon in a double Vodka!*
1) D.E.
2) B.C.D.E.
3) A.B.C.
4) E.

Wounds
To help a wound to heal – **Sanicle**
To ease the pain of a healing wound – **Marsh Mallow**
ALSO
(See; **Beech, Dittany of Crete, Elm**)

Yarrow (*Achillia millifolium*)

June – Nov. Venus.

<u>Colds & 'Flu</u>; *Mix equal parts of Yarrow, Pennyroyal, Sage, Catnip, Spearmint, Verbena, Horehound. Infuse 1 teaspoon in a covered cup for 10 mins. Take warm, every four hours. (Promotes sweating).*

<u>Burns & Scalds</u>; *Decote 1 tablespoon in a cup of olive oil for 20 mins. Strain and allow to cool. Apply to the affected part as a lotion.*

1) D.E.
2) B.C.D.E.
3) B.C.D.
4) E.

WORTCUNNING
A Folk Magic Herbal

First North American Edition, 2020
First Printing, 2020
ISBN 978-0-7387-6590-7

Originally published by Troy Books Inc. 2018
ISBN 978-1-909602-33-5

Llewellyn Publications is a registered trademark of Llewellyn Worldwide Ltd.

Cataloging-in-Publication Programme data is on file with the British National Bibliography.

Llewellyn Worldwide Ltd. does not participate in, endorse, or have any authority or responsibility concerning private business transactions between our authors and the public.

All mail addressed to the author is forwarded but the publisher cannot, unless specifically instructed by the author, give out an address or phone number.

Any Internet references contained in this work are current at publication time, but the publisher cannot guarantee that a specific location will continue to be maintained. Please refer to the publisher's website for links to authors' websites and other sources.

Llewellyn Publications
A Division of Llewellyn Worldwide Ltd. 2143 Wooddale Drive
Woodbury, MN 55125-2989 www.llewellyn.com

Printed in the United States of America

Contents

INTRODUCTION
A Folk Magic Herbal

n this section of the book I have taken the exact same plants that are given in the reverse section of this work and here give their traditional, magical usages. This information was not included in the original notes I received from the family of witches, so I have no way of knowing how they utilised herbs for their magical practice, or indeed if they even did. However, I feel that this information should be included in a book of this type and have therefore endeavoured to fill this omission with the traditional folk-magical uses of the herbs previously described medicinally. As this is intended to be a pocket-sized volume, for quick reference and usage, due to the limitations of space I have not been able to give encyclopaedic information on each herb. My aim here is to give the reader guidance on what herbs to use for what purposes and then they may research further if they need to; I give what I hope

are adequate references in the bibliography, for further study.

However, a quick word needs to be said here about the different types of suggestions that I make for the usage of the various herbs. I mention using the herbs in various ways; poppets or images, charm bags or sachets, teas/infusions or washes and incenses. I would here like to give a brief description of each of these methods for those who are new to this subject, or have not used herbs in this manner before.

Poppets. Otherwise known as Dolls, Dollies, Babbies or various other terms. These are generally a human shape that is cut out of a piece of cloth, felt or leather, two sides being sown together to create a hollow into which various objects may be inserted. The image is generally decorated or formed into the likeness of the intended subject of the magical working, and then magically/ritually identified with them. It is into the hollow that the herbs used may be stuffed, along with any other things appropriate to the type of magic being performed. Alternatives to fabric or leather are clay or wax, which may also have the herbs incorporated into their substance while being shaped. Another

method is to make the image from the herb itself, either carving the likeness from or into the root or branch, or forming a bundle of the herb into the correct shape and "dressing" it appropriately. An excellent (in my opinion, the definitive) guide to this form of magic is "Effigy", by Martin Duffy (details in the bibliography).

Charm Bags/Sachets. These items are either small, drawstring bags or pouches made of a natural material, such as felt, cotton, linen or leather or alternatively a flat piece of the same material, folded and tied up into a pouch. They are filled with the magically activated herbs and/or other items and either placed somewhere to do their work, or carried upon the person for specific reasons. In the past, many other materials were used for charm bags, such as horns and shells, even hollow rings, but cloth or leather is the more usual form these days.

Teas/Infusions & Washes. This form of magical working involves taking the herb, or herbs , required and soaking them in a liquid for a period of time. When ready, the liquid is strained off for magical use and the herbal material is discarded – usually in a ritual manner, such as an offering. The

liquid may be water, just like in making a cup of normal tea (especially if it is to be taken internally), but many other liquids may be used, depending on the purpose of the spell. Other mediums include vinegar, wine, alcohol/spirits, beer, rain sea or spring water and urine. The resultant liquid is magically charged and then used in an appropriate manner. It may be sprinkled or sprayed around a person, item or area; an item or person may be washed in it; it may be added to a ritual bath or used in any other way considered useful by the operator involved. Obviously, if drinking the infusion, ensure that it is safe to do so!

Incense. An incense is either a single herb, a combination of herbs, or a mixture of herbs, resins, essential oils and other materials, which are combined together and then usually burnt on charcoal. Other forms are incense sticks, usually known as Joss, or Cones, which is the material formed into a domed-type shape, and these are usually self-burning and do not need to be placed on charcoal. Incense can be used in many ways; to call or banish spirits; as an offering to deities; to create an atmosphere for ritual; to act as an aid to materialisation for a spirit or

deity, to cleanse and purify a person, place or thing; to empower and magically charge an item, charm, talisman or tool and for many other purposes.

The manner and ways in which herbs and plant material can be used by a magical practitioner are only limited by their imagination and personal skills; the sky is literally the limit. Do not limit yourself to the accepted correspondences either; if you do not have the herb that is given in the lists for your particular need, look at what you have available. The rule is always; use what you have. As for the morality of using them for and in any given situation, I will leave that for the reader to decide; but remember, it is not in the interests of any serious magical practitioner to deliberately harm anyone without good cause.

Nigel G. Pearson,
Suffolk, England.
Midsummer 2018.

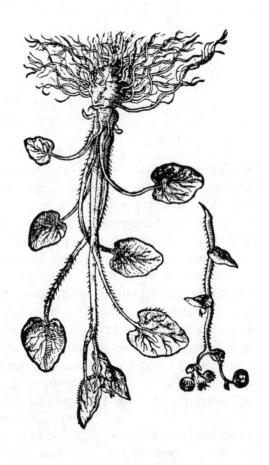

WORTCUNNING
A Folk Magic Herbal

❧ A ❧

Aconite (*Aconitum napellus*)
Saturn.
Monkshood, Wolfsbane, Stormhat, King's Coach, Thung.
Said to have been created by the Greek Goddess Hecate from the foaming saliva of Kerberos, the triple-headed dog which guards the gates of the Underworld. She placed it on Earth for the use of Her followers and it may be used, sparingly, in incense form to invoke Her presence. Famously used in malevolent magics and one of the ingredients found in old recipes for Flying Ointments and for elixirs taken to promote psychic vision and work. Although it may, indeed, be used in this manner, it is highly poisonous and the effective dose for ingestion is perilously close to the lethal dose. Unless you have expert knowledge and/or tuition, it is advised that you do not

use Aconite in this manner. It is far better employed in the form of a weak infusion and used as a wash for magical blades, or as an incense to cleanse them. This not only consecrates them to the magical arts, but also endows the power of protection and magical awareness, which guards all rituals in which the implement is used, against any intrusive or negative forces. This effect can also be utilised by including the dried plant in any charm bags or poppets intended to guard, ward and protect. One to use with caution and care.

Agrimony (*Agrimonia eupatoria*)
Jupiter.
Sticklewort, Agramie, Cockeburr, Church Steeples.
Deriving from the Greek word Argemone, meaning a white speck in the eye, Agrimony has long been held to be a very magical plant. It has been used as a ward against all wounds, snake bites, warts and other skin blemishes and was an ingredient in an infusion used to heal damage from hand guns. It is useful to cause sleep in a victim, as is detailed in an Old English medical text; "If it be leyd under mann's heed, He shal sleepyn as he were deed; He shal never drede ne wakyn, Till under his

heed it be takyn." These days it is of much more use in sleep pillows, perhaps with the addition of Hops, for sleep incubation and divinatory dreams. It can also be used in combination with Mugwort for various forms of psychic cleansing and healing. It is a useful herb for acts of counter magic and defence and is known to repel all works of malefic witchcraft. Interestingly though, it was also often used as a food for witches familiars.

Alder (*Alnus glutinosa*)
Venus.
Aller, Orle, Waller, Whistlewood.
The Alder is magically associated with the Underworld, with the Faere Folk and with the vital elements of Fire and Water. All of these make it an exceedingly powerful tree, but one of which to be wary. It is considered unlucky to unnecessarily cut an Alder, being protected by the Fay, as it is dangerous to attract their attention. They are known to very much favour the green dye obtained from its leaves and they do not take kindly to intervention from humans for no reason. The fact that it "weeps blood" when cut binds it very closely to the mythos and magic of the dying and resurrecting Gods

and those energies of life and fire in the Underworld. Its close association with water also links it with the Underworld, as rivers, streams, wells and lakes have always been viewed as entrances and crossing places to the Otherworlds and gifts of propitiation were cast into the waters of these places. Using an Alder whistle or flute can conjure up a strong wind or storm, which may equally be used for benefit or harm. However, using Alder wood as an incense can help dissolve harmful energies and disperse malevolent forces; using it without care however can cause dissension, even between the closest of friends. Hanging a branch of Alder in your home will bring it and you under the protection of powerful spirits, which can both attract good fortune and dispel negative forces. The bough is best picked around October, when both cones and catkins are present, representing the balance of opposing forces in control.

Alder Buckthorn (*Frangula alnus*)
Saturn.
Black Dogwood, Frangula Bark.
Overshadowed by its better-known namesake, the true Alder, the Buckthorn is little used

magically in general, although Dioscorides mentions the same use for cut boughs; i.e. that of hanging them up by windows and doors for protection against sorceries and enchantments. Another Greek, Galen the Physician, recommends this plant for protection against witchcraft, demons, poisons and headaches. However, one specific use of Buckthorn has been handed down, which goes as follows. Beneath the light of a Full Moon, take 3 handfuls of powdered Buckthorn and scatter it in a circle. Step inside the circle and begin to dance in a round, taking care to be fully aware at all times. At one point, an Elf will appear fleetingly and, before it disappears, you must stop dancing and declaim, "Halt thee and grant my boon!" If you manage this before the Elf flees, it will be bound to grant you one wish before it goes. The trick is in actually seeing the Elf first.

Angelica (*Angelica archangelica*)
Sun.
Archangel, Masterwort, Holy Ghost/Holy Ghost Plant.
One of the most powerful protective plants available. Widely used for its properties in the Pagan world, it was

"re-dedicated" to the Archangel/Saint Michael, after the coming of Christianity, as he was the guardian of the gates to the Underworld and a staunch protector against the forces of Darkness. It's use wards against all negative energies, spells and enchantments and, moreover, brings positive energy into one's life, manifesting as good fortune. Traditionally flowering on 8th. May, the feast day of St. Michael, it is a highly scented plant and gives off a pungent aroma when included in any incense. Lifting the spirits by its scent, it can be used in charm bags and sachets, made into infusions and drunk, or used in ritual bathing. It has long been used as a visionary herb, aiding the ability to see into other realms and worlds and, of course, is an excellent aid in communicating with the Archangel Michael.

Asafoetida (*Ferula assa-foetida*)
Saturn.
Devil's Dung, Food of the Gods.
A plant that is originally native to Afghanistan and widely used in Asian cookery, it is probably one of the most adulterated herbs on the market. Mostly

used in dried and powdered form, it is often mixed with wheat flour, clay, sand or gypsum, to bulk it out, so beware when buying that you have only the pure herb for magical use. It has an extremely bitter taste and a vile smell, which has been known to bring on vomiting in some people, but has been used for centuries to banish negative energies, malignant spirits and daemonic forces. It is often used in small quantities in incense, both to banish, but also to bind and control spirits under ritual conditions. In folk-magic, it is mostly used in charm bags or pouches that are worn about the body for protection, repelling spirits and for protection against illness, although this gives the bearer a decidedly queer odour. It is sometimes used in the darker magics for acts of cursing, by casting the powder on the ground in the direction of your enemy, or where they will walk across it, whilst reciting your curse. As one of its alternative names implies, it can be used as offerings to the male Gods of a more phallic, earthy or chthonic nature. It can be used in rites of exorcism and banishes manifestations of unwanted spirits if thrown on the charcoal during ritual.

Ash (*Fraxinus excelsior*)
Sun.
Nion.

Along with the Oak and Thorn, Ash is one of the most magical of trees and is included in the nine woods that make the Beltane fire. Ash twigs bound together into a faggot make an acceptable alternative to the Yule log and a miniature one can be kept in the house all year round as a blessing. Long prized for its strong, straight limbs, it is frequently used for wands and staffs and the traditional witches stang is often said to be made of Ash wood. Although also used for works of protection, the Ash is primarily used for magical healing rites. Warts may be removed by pricking them with a new steel pin or nail and inserting it into a "Maiden" Ash tree (one that is self-sown), whilst reciting the charm; "Ashen tree, Ashen tree, Pray buy these warts off me." A child with a hernia may be cured by splitting an Ash sapling vertically and passing the child through. The sapling is then bound up and as it heals, so shall the child. Ash wands are used in "stroking" magic for healing, passing the wand over the affected area many times whilst reciting the healing charm. Attach a lock of a child's hair to an Ash tree and it will

be cured of the whooping cough. To protect a newborn babe from ill-wishing, smear the honey made from Ash blossom on its lips, or the sap which oozes from a burning Ash twig. Ash may be used in charms for prosperity too; take a large bunch of Ash "keys" (the seeds) and keep these about the house or person and you will never want for money. According to folk-lore, snakes cannot abide Ash and will stay away from anyone carrying a wand of it, or will not be able to escape if surrounded by a circle of Ash twigs (go easy on this one!). Using a female Ash tree (sheder), will counteract the curses of a male witch and using the male Ash (heder), will work against those of a female witch.

🌿B🌿

Balm/Lemon Balm (*Melissa officionalis*)
Moon.
Garden Balm, Sweet Balm, Melissa, Bee Balm.
The word "Balm" is an abbreviation of "Balsam", referring to the sweet-smelling oil of this plant. "Melissa" is the Greek term for a Bee and this plant is much loved by them. Essentially a herb that is used in love magic, because of its calming and attracting qualities,

it also has great healing properties. It can be used in incenses for attracting a lover into one's life, or worn as a charm next to the skin. It makes a wonderful addition to a magical bath, the lemon-scented steam rising to the Gods and carrying your prayers for your soul-mate with it. Several of the leaves can be soaked in a cup of wine and shared as a loving-cup to strengthen a relationship, or offered to the Gods of love as a libation. As a magical healing herb, it is used for cleansing and closing wounds and, again, for its scent, which can uplift even the most depressed of spirits. Rub against your beehives to attract new bees and increase their production of honey and beeswax.

Basil (*Ocimum basilicum*)
Mars.
Sweet Basil, St. Joseph's Wort, Witches Herb.
As a herb of Mars, Basil is ideally used to promote courage and strength, both in yourself and others. Burning the herb as an incense before some particularly onerous or daunting task, or carrying the herb in a charm bag, will strengthen the will and fortitude of the bearer. Placing a couple of leaves in your shoe ensures you will never be short of money. To grow a Basil plant in your garden guarantees that you

will never lack admirers of the opposite sex and rubbing it on your skin soothes the worst of arguments between lovers. To divine if your love is true, place a Basil leaf in their hand; if it remains fresh, they are to be trusted, if it curls and withers, then find another. Strewing Basil leaves on the floor prevents any negative or malignant spirits entering your home and it can also be burnt in exorcism incenses. This is a herb that is also used to honour the dead as it is considered in folklore to open the gates of heaven; place on graves in remembrance of your ancestors and burn as an offering to their spirits to honour them. Basil is loved by Salamanders and Dragons, but hated by Scorpions – and Goats! The scent of this plant is considered regal in nature and is exalting to both the body and spirit.

Beech (*Fagus sylvatica*)
Saturn.
Queen of the Woods, Bok, Buke, Fagos.
Etymologically speaking, the words "Beech" and "Book" come from the same linguistic origin, being connected with writing materials and letters. Beech, then is good for all matters relating to knowledge and learning and acquiring the same. Use Beech

wood for making talismans and amulets for gaining information and intellectual growth. Rune and Ogham sets may be made from slips or slices of Beech, which, as a nut-bearing tree, is traditionally the type of wood that should be used for these oracles. A staff from Beech is a good thing to take on a quest for knowledge and sheltering under one is traditionally said to protect the traveller and also to ward off snakes. Take a stick of Beech and scratch or carve your desire on it, bury it under a leafing Beech tree and your wish will come to fruition. Keep the wood or leaves about you to increase your creative powers. Although nuts are generally considered to be promoters of fertility, Beech Mast (Nuts), can be used to promote fertility of the Mind instead of the body; string them on fine twine as a bracelet or prayer beads and use them to improve brain-power.

Bergamot (*Monarda didyma*)
Mercury.
Scarlet Mop, Bee Balm, Oswego Tea.
Not to be confused with the Bergamot plant which produces the oil for Earl Grey Tea (Citrus bergamia), or the "Bergamot Orange" (Mentha citrata), this is a herb originating

in North America, where a tea used to be commonly made from the young leaves. Its main magical use is in incense or infusions, used to relax and clear the mind of all intrusions, prior to serious occult work. It is also used to open up the higher faculties of the mind in preparation for all forms of clairvoyant, psychic and visionary work. Alternatively, a few leaves or flowers can be carried in the pocket to attract good fortune in daily life.

Bilberry (*Vaccinium myrtillus*)
Venus.
Whortleberry, Heather-berry, Hurts, Black Whortles, Whinberry, Huckleberry.
This low-growing, wiry shrub which is found widely in heathland and mountainous areas, produces a small, dark fruit which has been used medicinally since at least Anglo-Saxon times. The dried berries are used magically, mainly in charm bags. These can be carried about the body to bring good fortune and luck. They are also used in the turning back of hexes and in breaking curses; put nine, fresh berries in a small pouch if you think you have been the subject of ill-wishing – as the berries dry out, so will the curse be removed and sent back from whence it came.

The dried leaves can also be used in dream and wish magic. If you burn the leaves as an incense in the room in which you sleep, directly before you go to bed, your dreams of that night will come true. Results should be seen within a quarter moon (i.e. seven days), but the trick is in holding what you desire in your mind as you drift off to sleep, so that you will dream of it that night.

Birch (Silver) (*Betula pendula*)
Venus.
Lady of the Woods, Berke, Beth, Bouleau.
This beautiful, slender tree has a long magical history. It's name is anciently derived from an Indo-European root meaning "a tree whose bark is used for writing upon", and also shares the meaning of "brightness". This gives a clue to its magical uses. Apart from being a name of one of the Rune forms (Berkana/Beorc), with all the associations that that carries, it is used in protective charms against evil spirits, bad luck and the evil eye. Conversely it is also used in spells for fertility and love. For protective purposes, make a small "broom" or whisk from a handful of Birch twigs and use them to sweep around the edge of your property or

home, symbolically (and literally), sweeping out the ill luck. "Beat the bounds" at any liminal points, such as windows and doors and cast the ill back and away. To tap into the nurturing and romantic nature of this tree, use strips of the bark (carefully removed from the tree), as writings surfaces for spells and charms, which may then be buried at the foot of the tree with libations. Burn the wood as an incense in rites of romance. A birch tree decorated with strips of red and white cloth outside a stable will protect the horses inside from being "Hag-ridden" and sprigs of Birch twigs hung around the home will prevent domestic mishaps.

Boneset (*Eupatorium perfoliatum*)
Saturn.
Thoroughwort, Crosswort, Agueweed.
This native of North America is used for protection and exorcism. Make a strong infusion from any or all parts of the plant and sprinkle this around the house or person affected. This can also be used as a wash for items that you think have been tainted by malignity or ill-wishing; afterwards, pour the liquid out on the ground in full sunlight, to banish the malign influences.

Borage (*Borago officionalis*)
Jupiter
Burrage, Cool Tankard, Bugloss, Bee-Bread, Herb of Gladness.

This short, rough, hairy/spiky plant with bright-blue flowers is intimately concerned with courage and lightening of the spirits, because of its tonic effect on the heart and nervous system. There are various derivations of its name, including the Celtic "Barrach" (a man of courage) and from the Latin, "Ego Borago, Gaudia semper ago" (I, Borage, Bring always courage), but all revolve around this bolstering

of bravery. Magically it is mainly used in the form of a drink (tea, or infused in wine or ale), prior to testing rituals of endurance, initiation or strength. It may also be used in a ritual bath or burnt as an incense. Its alternate use is to aid in psychic vision and in visionary journeys; in this case an infusion should be made of the leaves and drunk a short while prior to the attempt. Carrying the fresh blossoms or wearing them in your buttonhole both protects and strengthens you on long journeys as well and planting them in your garden will attract that magical creature, the Bee.

Broom (*Cytisus scoparius*)
Mars.
Genista, Besom, Broom Tops, Basam, Brum, Green Broom.
Despite its beautiful, bright yellow flowers, the Broom plant has a mixed reputation, magically speaking. Its fine, whippy stems have been used in making besoms for centuries and because of it's brightness, these have been used to brush and banish ill-luck and misfortune away. It has been used in garlands and wreaths for weddings and handfastings, tied with ribbons, as a sign of joy and gladness. An infusion of the blossoms will also act to

exorcise spirits and poltergeists if sprinkled about the home. Conversely, as a plant of the Faere Folk, it is considered ill-luck to pick or disturb it in any way. An old Suffolk rhyme goes; "If you sweep the house with blossomed Broom in May, You are sure to sweep the head of the house away." A curse is said to follow whoever picks the blossoms for mere decoration, but it is fine to use them for sacred purposes. Witches, however, spurn mere superstition and readily use the plant in magic. To raise the winds, fling the blossoms into the air whilst calling upon the spirits of the Aires on a high hillside or mountaintop; to lay them again, burn the blossoms to ashes and bury them with whispered charms of cessation.

Burdock (*Arctium lappa*)
Venus.
Lappa, Fox's Clote, Beggar's Buttons, Burrs, Cockle Buttons, Gypsy Rhubarb.
The sticky burrs of this plant are well known to country folk and walkers, who find them a pain to remove, particularly from animals fur, but this gives a clue to the main magical use of Burdock, which is protective. The genus name Arctium, derives from the Greek "Arktos",

a Bear and "lappa" means "to seize", which bodes well for defensive properties. The root should be gathered on the Wane of the Moon and used in one of two ways. It may be used whole, carved into the likeness of a vaguely human-shape (do not use an iron knife!), dried and carried about the person as a protective amulet. Charms may be whispered to gain the protection of its residing spirit first. Alternatively, the root may be dried, chopped into equal-sized pieces, strung on red thread and worn as a protective necklace. The dried leaves may be used as a purifying and protective incense for the home and ritual area.

Burnet (*Pimpinella saxifraga*)
Sun.
Salad Burnet, Burnet Saxifrage, Lesser Burnet.
Not to be confused with the Great Burnet (Sanguisorba officionalis), with which it shares many habits, but this plant is much smaller and more slender. Well known for the usage of its leaves in Summer salads and cooling drinks, this Burnet also has valuable magical uses. As an incense, it is known to drive away problems of despair and depression, hence raising the spirits and enlivening the mind. However, it is as an infusion, or wash that

it is most valuable. When making your own magical tools, wash the separate parts with Burnet before assembling them; this not only purifies the tool for magical use, but also focuses and concentrates strong currents of force within it, which will then be released during the rituals it is used in.

🌿 C 🌿

Carrot (*Daucus carrota*)
Mars.
Philtron, Bird's Nest.

This common, kitchen vegetable has a long and venerable history in love and sex magic. The native, wild carrot is much smaller, more woody and spindly than the later cultivated variety, also being more white in colour, but the roots, seeds and ferny tops have been taken for centuries to promote both lust and fertility. The seeds are used to help women get pregnant and the root is eaten

to promote lustful thoughts. An alternate method is to use the dried root as a poppet, or mannikin, to bring two people together. Find two roots that resemble a male shape and a female shape (you know what I mean); bind these together, "face to face" and hang them up to dry – as they dry, the two people will be drawn to each other and into each others arms (or beds!). At the end of September each year, on the Scottish island of Uist, a festival was held, called "Carrot Sunday". The women of the island would go out and gather bunches of wild carrots, which they would then string together and sing songs in praise of "Michael the brave" and "Bride the fair" (St. Michael and St. Bridget), requesting their aid in fertility. Forked roots were especially sought for and prized.

Catnip (*Nepeta cataria*)
Venus.
Catmint, Nepeta, Field Balm, Nip.
Well known to be adored by felines, hence some of its names, old folk healers simply called this plant "Herba Cateria". Using this plant by feeding it by hand to your cat can cause a strong psychic bond between the two. If using the form of any feline when

astrally-projecting or shape-shifting, Catnip is of great value when taken as an infusion or used as incense. It can also be mixed with Dragon's Blood in an incense and used to exorcise oneself of bad habits. The incense can also be used devotionally by those who honour the Egyptian Powers Bast and Sekhmet. The main, magical use however, is in love and friendship spells. This herb can be combined with Rose petals in charm bags and sachets and used to promote love. If you hold a Catnip leaf in your hand and keep it there until it is really warm, then hold hands with someone, they will be your friend for life (as long as you always keep the leaf safely hidden). Grown near the door of the home, or hung above it, Catnip attracts benevolent spirits to your house and great good fortune too.

Centaury (*Centaurium erythraea*)
Sun.
Feverwort, Gentian, Centaury, Christ's Ladder, Bloodwort, Earth Gall.
Associated with the legendary centaur Chiron of Greek myth for its marvellous healing properties, this herb has been greatly venerated historically and was much used

by the Anglo-Saxons, who called it "Earth Gall". It had a high reputation to mediaeval magicians and it is listed in "Le Petit Albert" as one of fifteen magical herbs; "The eleventh hearbe is named........of Englishmen, Centaury.......this herbe hath a marvellous virtue, for if it be joined with the blood of a female Lapwing, or Black Plover, and put with oile in a lampe, all that compass it about shall believe themselves to be witches, so that one shall believe of another that his head is in heaven and his feete on earth; and if the aforesaid thynge be put in the fire when the starres shine it shall appeare yt the sterres runne one agaynste another and fyghte." Probably not a good idea to use it in this manner now though. Centaury's magical effectiveness may still be found in its use as an incense, whereby it increases psychic powers and encourages trance-like states. Its fumes are said to be able to drive away snakes and carried in a charm bag it is considered to be an excellent protection against all forms of malignant energy.

Chamomile (*Anthemis nobilis*)
Sun.
Maythen, Manzanilla, Whig Plant, Ground Apple.

Much used in herbal medicine for its calming properties, Chamomile has long been associated with sleep and banishing nervousness, as well as its noted anti-inflammatory actions. Magically, its uses are similar. Planted in the garden it can act as a Guardian herb Spirit to protect the property and ward off evil influence, both physical and energetic. Cast around the house, it removes any curses or spells sent against you. Included in an amulet or charm pouch, it brings success to any endeavour, particularly gambling, in which it brings good luck and attracts money. An infusion added to a ritual bath can bring success in the pursuit of love.

Chestnut (Sweet). (*Castanea sativa*)
Jupiter.
Sardian Nut, Jupiter's Nut, Husked Nut, Spanish Chestnut.

The wood of this tree is prized for its beauty and is used in many crafts, particularly furniture making and would make a beautiful wand or staff, however, there is little magical lore attached to this plant. The only use in this area that I can discover, is in love spells, in which only the nuts are used. You may

feed them to a prospective lover/partner to kindle amorous feelings towards you, or place them in charm bags to initiate the same feelings. Hanging them up on a string will create loving feelings in the home and ward against harsh words.

Chickweed (*Stellaria media*)
Moon.
Starweed, Starwort, Adder's Mouth, Hen Bite, Bird's Eye, Murren.
This prolific plant, which grows on practically all types of soil, derives its "Star" names from the shape of its small, white flowers, which it bears for most of the year. It might be thought then, that the lore of this plant would be associated with the skies or planets, but not so. It is a very homely plant, being a standard food for many animals – particularly domestic fowl – and is used in spells to attract, but mostly to maintain, love. Used dried in charm pouches, it has a similar effect to Chestnut, but is used more to create fidelity in a partner and maintain a loving relationship, than create one. It can be used as an infusion in a loving cup and is good to use in early spring to "freshen" any relationship when shared.

Cinquefoil (*Potentilla reptans*)
Jupiter.
*Five-fingers, Synkefoyle, Raven's Foot, Gooseweed,
Pentaphyllon, Moor Grass.*

A small, low-growing plant with creeping
habit, bearing yellow flowers on single stems,
the name refers to the fact that it bears
leaves divided into five, individual leaflets. If
you happen to find one with seven leaflets,
you should place it under your pillow to
dream of your future partner. A favourite
of the true Romany peoples, this plant has
a reputation for being a bit of a magical
jack-of-all-trades. Its most famous use is
in the historical witches Flying Ointments,
along with various other more narcotic
herbs and carriers such as pigs lard, soot and
baby's fat. It has strong sedative properties,
which lends itself to trance like states, but is
harmless on its own. Traditionally, the plant
is best collected either on a Waxing or Full
Moon, at midnight, as the day turns from
Wednesday to Thursday. It may be hung up
above the door or placed under the bed for
calm sleep and protection. An infusion of
the whole plant may be used as a wash to
rinse the forehead and hands nine times, to
rid oneself of hexes and curses. Carrying a

pouch of Cinquefoil gives one eloquence and a silver tongue when asking for favours from those in power; it is therefore often carried during court cases.

Coltsfoot (*Tussilago farfara*)
Venus.
Foalfoot, Coughwort, Son-before-father, Bullsfoot, Horsehoof.
Most names of this plant derive from the fact that the leaves resemble a horse or foal's foot. The strange-sounding alternative, "Son-before-the father", refers to the fact that, unlike most plants, the flowers emerge before the leaves in the early Springtime. Long used as a remedy for coughs and chest complaints, Coltsfoot is the only, or the main, ingredient in "British Tobacco". Whilst this is ostensibly used for medical complaints, magical workers have long used this smoking mixture to promote trance like states and also as an incense for visionary journeys. (Heavy and/or prolonged use of the herb in this form is not advised, as it contains types of alkaloids which may be damaging to the liver; small amounts over short periods may be used safely). In dried form, the herb is added to charm bags and

sachets for love magic and is also employed in spells for peace and tranquillity.

Comfrey (*Symphytum officinale*)
Saturn.
Knitbone, Bruisewort, Boneset, Yalluc, Ass Ear, Slippery Root.

The sovereign remedy for all forms of breaks, sprains bruises and wounds, as well as a rich source of vitamin B12. As with Coltsfoot, Comfrey contains alkaloids that may be toxic to the liver if taken in large amounts over a longer period, although eating a leaf or taking a cup of tea occasionally is perfectly safe. Magically speaking, Comfrey has always been used as a protective plant. It can be carried on the person in a charm bag, particularly when travelling, or used in an incense or "suffumigation" to smoke the traveller before setting out. This can be performed over pets and objects too if you wish to protect them or make sure they come back to you. Consecrating a protective talisman in Comfrey smoke would ensure the success of this charm. The herb, tucked into luggage, ensures that it comes back to you, should it become lost or stolen. The dried root is also used in money spells, to return lost funds and to attract extra income.

Couch Grass (*Witch Grass*) (*Agropyrum repens*)
Jupiter.
Witch Grass, Dog-grass, Twitch-grass, Scotch Quelch.
The bane of all gardeners, Couch Grass has small, spindly rhizome roots, which spread throughout an area and are exceedingly difficult to eradicate. Dogs will search out this root to eat if they feel sick, as it makes them vomit, hence getting rid of the poison in their stomachs. The roasted root has been used as a coffee substitute and the whole plant has been known and used since Greek and Roman times. Its magical virtues lie in its use for unhexing and getting rid of curses. An infusion of the whole plant may be sprinkled around the home or a person to banish unwanted spirits or energies and it may also be carried, fresh or dried in a charm bag, to lift depressive feelings. Sprinkled under the bed it may attract new lovers and refresh old ones.

Cowslip (*Primula veris*)
Venus.
Herb Peter/ St. Peter's Herb, Paigle/ Peggle, Palsywort, Fairy Cups, Our Lady's Keys, Plumrocks.
The original Anglo-Saxon term "cuslyppe"

actually means "cow-slime", and refers to the belief that this plant grew from cow dung. Considered the home of Elves and Faeries, the plant was dedicated to the goddess Freyja in ancient days, but became taken over by the Virgin Mary after Christianisation. Because of these associations, it was used in spells to beautify the complexion, as mentioned by Shakespeare in A Midsummer Night's Dream; "In their gold coats spots you see, These be rubies fairy favours, In those freckles lie their savours." Its other magical uses are as follows; if you do not wish to receive visitors, place Cowslip under the front porch and you will be left alone. Carry fresh Cowslip in a charm bag and it will preserve youthful looks, or restore them once lost. If looking for other things that are lost, hold a bunch of Cowslips in your hand and they will help you to find hidden treasures.

✓ D ✓

Dandelion (*Taraxacum officionale*)
Jupiter.
Lion's Tooth, Priest's Crown, Puffball, Swine's Snout, Witch Gowan, Piss-a-bed, Fairy Clocks.

Well-known to children for making you wet the bed if you pick it, Dandelion has long been used as a diuretic. It's other well-known usage is for telling the time, or your remaining age, by blowing the seed head and seeing what remains, or how many blows it takes to get rid of all the seed. (However, beware the old saw that says if you blow all the seeds off, then the child will be abandoned by its Mother). Magical uses are varied; drinking a tea made from an infusion of the root will bring on psychic powers. Leaving a steaming cup of this same tea beside the bed at night will call spirits to you. The plant, buried in the North-West corner of the house will bring favourable winds, and to send a message to a lover, blow the seed heads in their direction whilst thinking of the message. The dried flowers may be added to divination incenses and a wine made from the flowers is excellent for welcoming in the Summer tide.

Deadly Nightshade (*Atropa belladona*)
Saturn.
Banewort, Dwale, Devil's Cherries, Divale, Dwayberry, Belladonna, Poisonberry, Sorcerer's Berry, Witch's Herb.

All parts of this plant are toxic and are likely to be fatal if ingested in any but the smallest of quantities, so beware using this plant. Famed as an ingredient in the traditional Flying Ointment of mediaeval witches, the actual recipes remain closely guarded secrets. An incense containing the berries, and burnt in the open air, can be used in rites for contacting the Ancestors or the Departed, particularly at the Dark of the Moon, or All Hallows. A watery solution or tincture may be used to pour over certain fetishes in rain-making rites and the dried root carried about the person, is said to bring good fortune to gamblers. It is a plant easily attracted to negative or malevolent energies and, if desired, can be used to contact spirits of this nature for works of revenge or destruction. It may also be used in the same way as the famed root of the Mandrake plant, in that a spirit servant or Familiar may be bound to the root and used to do the witches (magical) bidding, as long as it receives sufficient care and payment. A magical ink can be made by infusing the crushed berries in vinegar; use for writing hexes curses and other spells. The remaining berries may be dried and used as incense

ingredients. It can be used as an offering, or as an incense, to call upon Hecate, Circe or Bellona and tradition says that it may only be picked, properly, for magical use on Walpurgisnacht, the Eve of May.

Dittany of Crete (*Origanum dictamnus*)
Venus.
Dittany.
The main use of this plant is as an incense. It is of great use to aid the manifestation of any spirits that you may wish to communicate with; they use the rising smoke as a medium in which to appear and to create a semi-solid body. In this manner it is often used at All Hallows to gain conversation with the spirits of the Ancestors, Kin and past Teachers and Guides, to receive knowledge, insight and wisdom. It is used as an offering to the Powers Persephone and Osiris, both of whom have Underworld functions and associations. As an incense, it is also said to aid in attempts at extra-corporeal travel and while breathing in its fumes, prophetic utterances may be made for group rituals. The juice of Dittany is said to be held in abhorrence by venomous beats, so smearing some about your person will keep them at bay.

Dock (*Rumex obtusifolias*)
Jupiter.
Common Dock, Butter Dock, Wayside, Herb Patience.

This is the plant whose leaves are well-known for relieving the severe itching of a Nettle sting; "Nettle in, Dock; Dock in, Nettle out; Dock rub, Nettle out!" Otherwise, it is the seeds of this plant that are of use in magic and they are either put into charm bags, or burnt as an incense to increase wealth and attract money. Made into an infusion, this may be sprinkled about a business to increase the flow of paying customers. Strangely enough, when the dried seeds of Dock are wrapped in one of its leaves and tied to the left arm of a barren woman, it is said that they will help her to conceive a child.

❧ E ❧

Elder (*Sambucus nigra*)
Venus.
Black Elder, Bourtree, Boontree, Whistle Tree, Pipe Tree, Faerie Tree, Hylder, Eldrum.

The Elder is a powerful plant on many levels and carries an ambiguous nature, perhaps this is why it is the witch tree par excellence. It is

sacred to the old, female Powers and lore tells us that it is frequently the abode of a goddess or is a witch shape-shifted. The cutting of its wood is a dangerous task and must be accompanied by offerings and the spoken charm; "Lady Ellhorn, give me some of thy wood, and I will give thee some of mine, when it grows in the forest." The wood can be made into protective charms, tied with red thread, but makes poor wands or staffs, as it is not very strong. The dried blossom may be used in incenses as a fixative for other ingredients, as it holds scent well and releases both its own and others back when burnt. Elder gives a boost of energy to anything it is used with, so is useful in any magical rite. The wood itself must never be burnt, but is useful in making magical whistles to call the spirits; hollow out the pith in the middle of small branches and cut holes for the notes. These should be used in the wild far from human habitation. The berries may be used (as well as the blossoms), to make a good red wine for the ritual Cup and to honour the female Powers, of whom the Elder is a strong embodiment. Use the berries to scatter over a person as a blessing and in front of a newly married couple when exiting the church. Never beat a child with an

Elder stick as it will wither and be sickly. Sit quietly beneath an old Elder on Midsummer's Eve, placing your back against it and sink into a meditative state. In this quiet reverie, visualise the trunk of the plant as being hollow and filled with steps leading down into the Underworld. Step down in your mind into the depths and you will see what you will see within the inner Faerie realms. Planted near a grave, Elder will protect the body from those who seek to dig it up for ill use.

Elecampane (*Inula helenium*)
Mercury.
Elf Dock, Elfwort, Scabwort, Horseheal, Velvet Dock.

 Another plant closely associated with the Elven/Faerie Folk, so one to treat carefully, as their attention is often a double-edged sword. It may be dried and ground down and offered as an incense to gain their attention, or merely as a gift. The incense may also be burned when scrying to help increase your

psychic vision. It is carried in charm pouches when setting out on long journeys to convey protection and is frequently an ingredient in love sachets, placed next to the body to attract a partner. Taken internally as an infusion, it is said to be able to heighten sensitivity to magical work and aid in its effectiveness. At all times use with care and respect for fear of antagonising the Elven Folk.

Elm (*Ulmus campestris*)
Saturn.
Elven, Elven-Elm.
One more plant closely associated with the Lordly Ones so, again, another to use warily. Mediaeval magicians were said to favour wands made from Elm and the Norse gods made the first woman from Elm (the first man came from **Ash**). It is a tree that calms the mind and aids in meditation, giving glimpses of the realms of the Plant Kingdom and Spirits, when sat beneath it. To receive prophetic dreams, prick an Elm leaf with a new pin, then place it under your pillow at night. Boughs of Elm are placed over doorways to protect the inhabitants from ill-luck or ill-wishing, especially stables or cow sheds. It is also used to protect from

lightening strikes and will draw love to the bearer when warn. Sadly now a rare tree, due to the devastations of Dutch Elm disease in the 1970's in Britain and now little seen.

Eyebright (*Euphrasia officionalis*)
Sun.
Meadow Eyebright, Euphrosyne, Red Eyebright.
A useful herb for clearing the mind of negativity and changing the attitude to a more positive one. Named for one of the Greek Graces, Euphrosyne, meaning "gladness", it lifts the spirits and gives the witch a clearer grasp on problems and situations. Taken as an infusion internally, or brushed onto the eyelids before working, it is said to increase natural psychic abilities and enable one to see to the heart of a matter and enable the necessary alteration in thought patterns to achieve success.

🐾 F 🌺

Fennel (*Foeniculum vulgare*)
Mercury.
Fenkel, Sweet Fennel, Seaside, Ferny-plant.
One of the sacred herbs in the Anglo-Saxon Nine Herbs Charm, tradition states that

it should never be cultivated for magical purposes, but taken directly from the wild, most properly on Midsummer's Eve; "Sow Fennel, Sow Trouble", as the old adage goes. Much used in magical infusions for courage and to strengthen resolve it is also said to be able to give long life and maintain fertility and virility; for this reason, it is also included in love charms and potions, or carried in sachets. Fennel's other main magical use is in its protective properties. It can be hung around the doors and windows to prevent the intrusion of malevolent spirits and pushing a few seeds or the ferny tops of the plant into the keyhole, will prevent the entry of angry ghosts. An infusion may be sprinkled around the ritual area or used in a bath for protective purposes and the seeds used in an incense will have the same effect. Placing a piece of Fennel in your left shoe wards you from danger when on a long journey.

Feverfew (*Tanacetum parthenium*)
Venus.
Featherwort, Flirtwort, Bachelor's Buttons, Featherfoil, Nosebleed, Midsummer Daisy.
Carrying Feverfew will protect against colds, fevers and accidents. Dedicated to the

goddess Venus, Culpepper states that it had been provided by her to aid all womankind, so it is of especial use in woman's magic. Planted around the house it will cleanse the air and ward off noxious energies. The dried herb may be used in protective incenses to ward the home and ritual area and the burning plant also calms the mind for magical work, especially at Midsummer.

Foxglove (*Digitalis pupurea*)
Venus.
Witch's Gloves, Gloves of Our Lady, Deadmen's Bells, Cow-Flop, The Great Herb, Fox Bells, Fairy's Glove, Fairy Weed, Fairy Fingers, Fairy Caps.
This is a highly toxic herb if taken internally, but may be handled with care otherwise. From the plethora of folk names connected to it, this can be seen to be a plant of the Faere Folk par excellence, but this is again a double-edged sword. For those who wish to work with the Faerie you may proceed thus; create a full ritual circle in which to work. With a cup of the freshly expressed juice of Foxglove, trace a line from East to West and then another from South to North, such that they bisect in the centre. Once the circle is banished, the lines remain as an invitation to the Faerie Folk to visit, telling

them that the witch is of good intent. Planting the herb in the garden is a protection for both it and the home. To prevent evil from entering the house, a black dye is made from the leaves of the plant and used to paint crossed lines on the (stone) floor. It is said that the juice of Foxglove will restore a child that has been taken by the Faerie and it is, of course, the original source of the famous heart stimulant, Digitalin.

G

Garlic (*Allium sativum*)
Mars.
Poor Man's Treacle, Stinkweed, Ramsons, Devil's Posy, Gypsy's Onions.
Well known for its protective properties, this is a plant dedicated to the goddess Hecate, whom the Greeks used to honour by placing a clove on a small pile of stones at a crossing of roads. It is one of the ingredients included in the famous "Four Thieves Vinegar", used to banish and ward magically. Grown in the garden it protects the house from evil influence and the spells of black witchcraft. A rope of Garlic bulbs may be hung in the house to repel ill-wishing and thieves and a bulb, placed under a child's pillow at night,

will protect its sleep. Sailors carried Garlic to prevent their ships from being wrecked and Brides carried a clove in their posy to bring good luck. Worn about the neck it protects against foul weather and monsters and will protect you from the blows of your enemies. It may be rubbed against any ailing part of the body, to absorb the evil influence, then cast into a West-flowing stream to banish the illness. To rob an enemy's magical lodestone of its powers, rub it with Garlic, then cast the herb away and to prevent evil spirits attacking you, bite into a whole bulb then breathe into their faces.

Gentian (*Gentiana lutea*)
Mars.
Felwort, Bitter Root, Bald Mary, Yellow Gentian.

This extremely bitter herb is, perhaps strangely, used in love magic. It can be added to baths taken before performing amatory magic, or washes used to clean the ritual tools, and added to sachets and charms

for the same effect. These must be given to your intended, without them knowing. It can be added to any incense or sachet, for any purpose, to give the work extra power. Powdered it can be used to cast around a haunted house for protection, or to break hexes and curses that have been cast in the vicinity. It was used in the past as a cure-all and was particularly favoured as an antidote to poison.

❦ H ❦

Hawthorn (*Crataegus laevigata/monogyna*)
Mars.
May, Whitethorn, Hagthorn, Bread and Cheese, Quickthorn, Awes, Azzies, Boojuns.
The Hawthorn is also one of the prime Faerie trees and is famed throughout the British Isles for this association. Many people will not uproot a Hawthorn for fear of angering the Faere Folk and many is the tale of disaster told if this has actually been done. The Hawthorn is often linked with the **Oak** and the **Ash** and, together, these trees are known as the Faerie Triad. Wherever they are found growing together is seen as a haunt of the Lordly Ones and a gateway to other worlds.

Magically, Hawthorn leaves can be chewed with intention to aid focus and Otherworldly contacts at sacred sites. Whereas the thorns from the tree, equally as sharp as those from the Blackthorn, can be used to pierce poppets for love magic and healing. Carrying the thorns in a pouch around the neck is thought to bring luck when hunting and fishing and a rosary of Haws can be used for meditative purposes or to count the number of chants used in a spell. The blossoms made into a wine can be used to toast the Lady of Love at the May rites and a wand made of the white, peeled wood may be used to control malevolent spirits and cast enchantments. Branches of May can be put up over the doors and windows, especially at Roodmass, to protect the house from ill-wishing and malevolent spirits. Bathing the face with dew from the Hawthorn on May Morning bestows beauty and enhances the complexion. Hawthorn also protects against lightening and no evil ghosts may linger in a house where it is present.

Hazel (*Corylus avellana*)
Mercury.
Halse, Hezzel, Ranger, Woodnut, Lambs tails, Hale.

The beautiful, straight shafts of Hazel lend themselves well to the making of magical wands and staffs, particularly so as it is seen as a symbol of wisdom and knowledge, conferring Otherworldly power on the bearer. Most water divining rods are made from Hazel, forked or not, and it is definitely a property of this magical wood that aids the "water witch" and not just a learnt technique. The wand must be cut at night on the Dark of the Moon (or a holy day in the Christian calendar); facing East, cut from the Eastern-facing branches of the Tree. The wand must then be shown to the rays of the rising Sun for a sealing blessing. An incense made from the leaves or twigs may be used for most magical purposes, as it strengthens the magical Will and aids focus and concentration and it is one of the nine sacred woods used for kindling magical fires. The nuts make good fertility charms or string them up in the house for good fortune. Sailors once wore sprigs of Hazel to protect them against shipwreck and driving three pins of the wood into the wall of your house will guard against fire damage. Wearing a "crown", woven from the twigs and new leaves, during ritual/magical

workings ensures their success and is also said to confer invisibility on the wearer.

Heartsease (*Viola tricolor*)
Venus.

Pansy, Love-in-idleness, Love-lies-bleeding, Butterfly Flower, Loving Idol, Cuddle-Me, Call-to-you, Herb Trinitatis, Bouncing Bet, Bullweed, Banwort, Banewort.

From the many folk names referring to love that this plant possesses, it is obvious that it's main use is in amatory charms; indeed it is the very herb that led to so much confusion in Shakespeare's great play, "A Midsummer Night's Dream". The dried petals/flowers may be used in charm bags or sachets and presented to the intended lover, or placed secretly near where they will walk over them. Chaplets or crowns may be magically prepared and given as gifts. The juice from the flowers may be used in magical love philtres and introduced into food or drink, or sprinkled over/around where the object of affection lives. Or simply, a posy of the flowers may be presented with magical intention to the object of affection. The term Banwort comes from the Anglo-Saxon banwyrt (bone plant), as it was thought good for healing broken bones.

Hemlock (*Conium maculatum*)
Saturn.
Herb Bennet, Hecklow, Humlock, Kex, Keckies, Beaver Poison, Poison Hemlock, Poison Parsley, Spotted Hemlock, Spotted Corobane.

A highly poisonous plant and a favourite means of execution in Ancient Greece, it was the herb taken by the philosopher Socrates to procure his death. Once used to induce astral projection, the difference between the narcotic and fatal dose is miniscule and so is not recommended as a travelling agent. Its magical uses these days are in the ritual preparation and consecration of bladed tools. The fresh juice may be (carefully), rubbed onto the metal parts of the weapons, to empower and sanctify them.

Hemlock Water Dropwort (*Oenanthe crocata*)
Saturn.
Cowbane, Water Hemlock, Dead Man's Fingers.
Frequently confused with common Hemlock and known as the most poisonous plant in Britain, it may be mainly distinguished from it in that the umbel of flowers is denser and more compact and it's stem is not spotted. The 17th century apothecary and reviser/updater of Gerard's Great Herbal, Thomas Johnson,

was concerned that apothecaries did not know enough about plants to avoid being supplied with the wrong ones by the women who gathered and sold them. He implies that this mistaken supply may not, always, have been an innocent error on behalf of the gatherers. He notes that Hemlock Water Dropwort is to be easily found at the Horse Ferry near Lambeth. The plant, he says, is often sold as peony. I have been unable to trace any, true, magical uses for this plant, but it was also used to execute criminals and the elderly who couldn't support themselves, in times past.

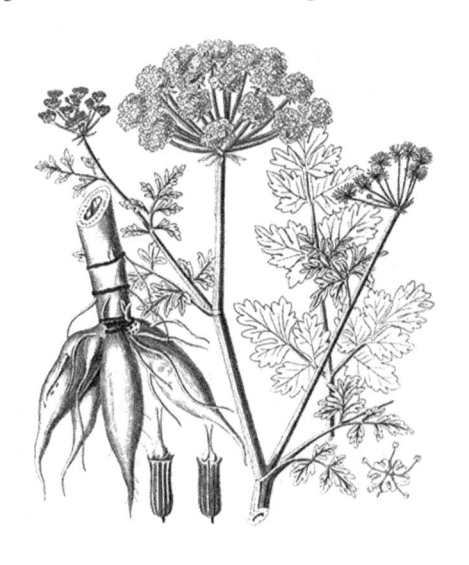

Henbane (*Hyoscyamus niger*)
Saturn.
Henbells, Toothwort, Symphoniaca, Jupiter-s Bean, Hog's Bean, Dog-Piss, Deus Cabballinus.
Another highly toxic herb, traditionally held to be one of the ingredients of the witches Flying Ointment. Certainly it has a sinister reputation as, in Greek mythology, the Dead were crowned with it as they wandered beside the River Styx. Charms of slices of dried Henbane root were hung around the necks of children, both to prevent fits and seizures and to cure the pain of toothache. The same charm, worn by adults, brings the love of the opposite sex. It's main use is in summoning the spirits of the Dead and working with the Ancestors, to which end it is used in incense form. Take dried Henbane, Frankincense, Fennel, Coriander and Cassia and grind to a fine powder. Take this to a dark and haunted forest at night and place on glowing coals on a tree stump. Surround this by lighted black candles and call on the Spirits. You will know when they arrive, as the candles will be suddenly snuffed out. When you have finished your communion, rid yourself of the Spirits by burning

Asafoetida and Frankincense. Great care should be taken with this operation and it should only be performed by one who is experienced in the magical arts. Alternatively, to raise a storm, cast the herb into boiling water, or to make it rain, throw it into a running stream. Poppets may be stuffed with Henbane leaves to deter trespassers on your property and the dried pods, once the seeds have been removed, may be used as magical containers for all types of Saturnian works.

Herb Robert (*Geranium robertianum*)
Venus.
Red Robin, St. Robert's Herb, Cranesbill, Fox Geranium, Bloodwort, Knife and Fork.
In the Middle ages, this herb was regarded as sacred to St. Robert but, as there are several of that name, it is not clear which one is meant, nor what particular properties were ascribed to it in that case. However, Robert, or its diminutive Robin, was/is a name used for the Horned God of the wild and the witches and so it is also considered as sacred to Him. It is also a Faerie plant and is especially associated with Hobgoblins. In rituals to honour or communicate with

65

any of these Beings, Herb Robert may be used as an incense, drunk as a tea prior to invoking them, or worn as wreaths or garlands during the rites.

Holly (*Ilex aquifolium*)
Mars.
Holen, Hulver, Holme Oak, Bat's Wings, Holy Tree, Christ's Thorns.

Considered a strongly masculine plant (Ivy being the female equivalent), Holly has long been a sacred plant. It was used by the Druids in their winter rites and is one of the plants considered to have made the crown of thorns worn by Jesus. It is a protective plant par excellence, primarily used to keep intruders at bay, to deflect negative energies and rebound curses and ill-wishing on the sender. It makes a very effective boundary hedge around the home, both physically and magically, protecting all within. Holly may be used in charm bags and incense for all

defensive rites and bunches of it hung up at doorways and windows will prevent evil spirits from entering the home. Infused or distilled Holly water may be sprinkled on newborn babies to protect them and throwing a sprig after a runaway animal will make it return of its own accord. Fire, lightening and poison cannot exist in its presence and for this reason, door frames and windowsills were made of its wood in days gone by. After midnight on Good Friday morning, pluck nine, spineless leaves from a Holly bush and tie them up in a plain, white handkerchief with nine knots. Go back to bed and place this bundle under your pillow and your dreams of that night will come true. The berries are excellent for making magical rosaries/prayer beads from. Simply string them on a line of red thread and hang them up to dry. Use these for chants and spell counting, or leave them hanging up as decorative protective charms. The peeled wood of Holly is a beautiful, clean white and it makes excellent wands and staffs, which take to carving well once dried.

Hops (*Humulus lupulus*)
Mars.
Hop Bine, Willow Wolf, Beer Flower.

Named from the Old English hopen or hoppan, meaning "to climb", it derived its name of Willow Wolf from its leaves, which have the habit of twining around Willow trees in the wild. This shows its main, magical use as that of binding, constraining or holding. Taking some of the stem, use these to wrap around poppets or images of people you wish to hold or bind from doing something. Alternatively, use this plant to support or hold in things you wish to preserve. Long known for its use in flavouring beers and for its soporific values, it can be used in magical sachets or charm bags to induce sleep and healing while at rest. Sprigs of the plant may be hung up by the hearth to bless the house and assure an abundant supply of food and drink.

Horehound, White (*Marrubium vulgare*)
Mercury.
Hoarhound, Hune, Huran, Bull's Blood, Seed of Horus, Eye of the Star, Soldier's Tea.
Horehound is a great herb for clearing the mind and focussing intention. Burnt as an incense during ritual, it aids the "flow" of the rite and helps keep it all together. It protects from outside influences and wards off any negativity that may be in the way of success.

It is therefore a good protective plant and can be worn, carried or used in charm bags for defence against malefic witchcraft, evil spells and can break curses and hexes. It wards against harm when carried on journeys and is carried to guard against sorcery and fascination. An infusion will help clear the mind in preparation for any form of divination and helps you to see the results much better. An infusion of this herb is also useful during exorcisms and should be sprinkled around and over the person, place or thing affected.

Hyssop (*Hyssopus officionalis*)
Moon.
Isopo, Ysope.
Despite frequent allusions to it in the magical literature, this is very unlikely to be the same plant that is referred to in the Bible passage; "Purge me with Hyssop and I shall be clean" (Psalm 51:7). This plant is not native to the Middle East and did not grow there in Biblical times. The Biblical plant is almost certainly Origanum syriacum, which does grow in the Middle East, and is known as Ezov (Ezob) in Biblical Hebrew. However, time, practice, usage and tradition have shown that the two plants have similar, if not identical effects on

the material and magical/spiritual levels and may, therefore, be used interchangeably. The main usage of this herb is for purification/ protection and cleansing. It may be hung up in bunches around doorways, windows and other openings, to prevent the entry of noxious energies and spirits and also to banish them. Used as an infusion in a wash or a spray, it may be employed to cleanse areas and people of unwanted or unclean energies. As a wash it is used to cleanse and prepare magical tools for consecration and practical use, and it has long been used as an Asperger in magical rites. Simply cut a bunch of the herb when it is in flower, dry it, tie with red thread at the base (or tie it onto a suitable wooden handle), and use it to sprinkle consecrated water around a person, place or object. It way also be used in cleansing baths, preparatory to ritual work. Hyssop has also been used in love magic, to bind the object of affection to the operator.

🌿 J 🌿

Juniper (*Juniperis communis*)
Sun.
Ginepro, Enebro, Mountain Yew, Gin Berry, Horse Saver.

The main folk magical use for this helpful
plant is in its aromatic smoke when burned;
both berries and foliage may be used, dried
or fresh. It has been used for centuries as a
purificatory agent in the case of hauntings
and spirit possession, of ill health when
supernatural agencies were suspected and for
general ghostly hauntings and infestations. In
the Highlands of Scotland it was the custom
for the young men on Hogmanay (New Year's
Eve), to go into the hills and collect Juniper
branches, which would then be left out
overnight by the fire to dry. In the morning,
all the doors and windows would be closed,
the dried branches lit and the whole house
fumigated with the aromatic smoke. This was
to banish any lingering, negative influence
from the past year and to cleanse and purify
the home for the New Year just begun. It
is a highly protective herb, attracting fresh
energies and banishing negative ones. It may
be worn to protect against the evil-eye and
general ill-wishing and hung up in the home
for the same purpose. In addition, when
carried or burned, it increases one's one
psychic powers, at the same time as breaking
any hexes or curses cast against you. Juniper is
also associated with truth and justice and may

therefore be used in situations where these qualities need to be attracted, particularly in court cases. Carry a small pouch of 5 Juniper berries in your pocket and you will be successful in any legal case you may have (as long as you are in the right!).

L

Lady's Mantle (*Alchemilla vulgaris*)
Venus.
Lion's Foot, Leontopodium, Bear's Foot, Nine Hooks, Stellaria, Dewcup, Breakstone. Elfshot.
Anciently used magically and associated with various Earth Goddesses, this plant became associated with the Virgin Mary in the Middle Ages, hence "Lady's Mantle", not "Ladies Mantle". The shape of the leaves are said to resemble the scalloped edges of the Virgin's cloak and the dew that is collected in the leaves

in the morning is not only used as a magical face-wash to enhance the complexion but, more importantly, as an ingredient in many spells to enhance their efficacy. It is said that this dew will increase the power and focus the energy, particularly of the work of Alchemists, and will seal the power within it. The plant may also be carried to attract love and can be included in any ritual baths or magical sachets connected with this work. As this plant is particularly associated with the feminine, it is used for any problems affecting women and for men who wish to contact their feminine nature. In Ireland, this plant was used to combat the effects of "Elfshot" and heal the victim.

Larkspur (*Delphinium consolida*)
Venus.
Lark's Heel, Lark's Toe, Lark's Claw, Knight's Spur.
This is a toxic plant, particularly the seeds, which causes vomiting and purging if eaten and this gives the clue to its magical use. It has long been used to expel ghosts and unwanted spirits and, also, to purge the eyes of impediments. Hang the plant up (carefully), in the home to keep

away bad ghosts, or use the seeds in an incense to smoke the house and repel all negative sprites. Holding a bunch of Larkspur up before your eyes (again, carefully), and looking at the Midsummer fires through the leaves, will expel any impurities and keep them clean until the next Midsummer.

Lavendar (*Lavandula officionalis*)
Mercury.
Spike, Elf Leaf, Nard, Nardus.
A little-known part of the lore surrounding this ubiquitous plant involves the attraction and favour it has for the Faere Folk, hence one of it's common names. It is closely associated with the time of Midsummer, which is well-known for its Faerie associations and here is a method by which you may make their acquaintance – carefully! To make a Lavendar Wand, take nine strong stems of Lavendar, freshly cut from the garden (dried stems are too brittle), tie them tightly together with a long, narrow ribbon about four times the length of the stems, just under the flower heads. Now, double back the stems, one at a time and weave one end of the

ribbon between them. Nine, being an odd number, the warp of the stems should appear in alternate bands with the ribbon in cross threads. Continue weaving down to the bottom of the stems after you have completely enclosed the flowers heads inside the cage, then take both ends of the ribbon and tie them off together, round the end of the stems. You should now have a sweet smelling, fragrant Wand, that may be used in actuality when dealing with the Faerie Folk in Summer rites. As well as its attraction to the Fay, Lavendar is much used in incenses to raise vibrations to a higher, calmer, more peaceful level. It can be used in bags and sachets for love spells and it is said that inhaling its scent enables one to see ghosts. Spread Lavendar flowers around a room to cleanse it and to promote healing and friendship.

Linseed, (Flax) (*Linum usitatissimum*)
Mercury.
Mary's Linen Cloth.
Sacred to the Teutonic goddess Hulda/ Holda, who is said to have first taught mankind how to make its fibres into linen thread, and also the art of weaving, this

plant is intimately connected with the flows of Fate. Linen yarn may be used in cord and knot magic of all types, particularly in cases of fortune, luck and money. Tying the "luck" into the knots and hanging the charm up in the house will help the home to prosper, or untie the knots at times when you need extra finance. Carry the seeds in your purse or wallet to attract money and good fortune and, at the same time, ward off malefic witchcraft and the evil eye. To prevent evil from entering the home, take a small handful of flax seeds and wrap them up in a "twist" in a square of red paper; place this by the hearth and renew each year. If you wish to bless your child, at the age of seven, let them dance among the blue-flowering Linseed plants and they will forever be beautiful. Linseed oil may be used to consecrate divinatory tools, particularly items such as crystal balls and shew stones; beneath the light of a Full Moon, lightly coat the surface of the tool with oil and leave out overnight. The next morning, polish the surface brightly, then wrap the item in a red cloth and put away until needed. Never let it be exposed to direct sunlight again or its powers will be lost.

Liquorice Root (*Glycyrrhiza glabra*)
Venus.
Lycorys, Liquiritia, Lacris, Reglisse.
Some fifty times sweeter than sugar, the root of this plant has long been used in herbal medicine, and as a delightful treat for children of all ages. The roots of Liquorice have, in the past, been used as wands, being very long, tough and fibrous when dried. However, the main use of this plant is in love magic, to "sweeten" the chosen one's affections. The chopped root can be added to love and lust charm bags and sachets and in spells to ensure the fidelity of one's beloved. Chewing a piece of the fresh root, then kissing the object of your affections will ensure that your passions will be returned.

Loosestrife, Yellow (*Lysimachia vulgaris*)
Venus.
Yellow Willow Herb, Herb Willow, Willow-wort, Wood Pimpernel.
Its common name of Loosestrife is a very old one, and refers to the belief that the plant would quieten savage beasts, and that in particular it had a special virtue 'in appeasing the strife and unruliness which

falleth out among oxen at the plough, if it be put about their yokes.' For the same reason, the dried herb used to be burnt in houses, so that the smoke might drive away gnats and flies. It was particularly valuable in marshy districts. Snakes and serpents were said to disappear immediately the fumes of the burning herb came near them. Hanging up bundles of the herb will promote harmony and banish discord amongst the inhabitants of the house.

Lovage (*Levisticum officionale*)
Sun.
Lubestico, Love Root, Love Herb, Love Rod, Lavose, Sea Parsley, Italian Parsley, Cornish Lovage.
Infused in the water, Lovage is often used magically as a bathing herb. It gives its delicate scent to the bather and, in this manner, draws romance into one's life. Frequent bathing with this herb is said to enhance one's physical beauty but, moreover, to let the inner beauty shine out from within. The bath can be used before any ritual to purify the witch and the infusion may be used to cleanse any magical tools. Placing Lovage leaves inside the shoes is said to be able to revive and refresh after a wearying journey.

❦M❦

Mallow, Common/Tree/Marsh (*Common - Malva sylvestris; Tree - Lavatera arborea; Marsh - Althaea officionalis*)

Moon.

Mallards, Mauls, Schloss Tea, Mortification Root, Velvet Leaf.

Although different plants, all types of Mallow tend to be used interchangeably for magical purposes. It is much used in love and sex magic, being deemed highly aphrodisiacal; carrying a leaf or leaving a vase of the flowers outside your door makes a departed lover think of you and aids in his return. An ointment can be made by steeping the seeds (gathered at Full Moon), in vegetable oil and rubbing it on the genitals; this acts both as an aphrodisiac and is said to cure impotence. An amulet may be made from the root or leaf and kept near the genitals for the same purpose. In mediaeval tradition, binding a Mallow root wrapped in black wool to the thigh with linen thread, would protect a woman against ailments of the "teats". Mallow is also very protective against malefic witchcraft and ill-wishing; this time, steep the leaves in

oil and rub the resultant ointment into the skin. This preparation is also said to cast out devils. The seeds, which should always be gathered at the Full of the Moon, may be added to incenses designed for exorcisms, protection and to aid in journeys to the Otherworld.

Marigold (*Calendula officionalis*)
Sun.
Mary's Gold, Golds, Ruddes, Summer Pride, Gowles, Bride of the Sun, Oculus Christi.
A truly benevolent plant on all levels. It may be used to consecrate ritual tools, either in incense form, or with an oil made from the petals infused in sunflower oil. It is used for prophetic dreams by placing them beneath your pillow; your dreams will come true and you will uncover the thief who has stolen your property. Garlands of the flowers can be placed around the doorway to prevent the entrance of evil spirits and negativity and adding them to your bath water will bring you admiration and respect from all who meet you. It is said that the flowers give out sparks during thunderstorms and picking these blossoms at midday in the full sun will strengthen and gladden the heart. However,

pick a bunch of the blooms at dawn and you will turn into an alcoholic. Planting Marigold on the graves of your ancestors will bless their souls and keep them safe in the afterlife. Carrying a wolf's tooth which is wrapped in Marigold flowers collected in a ritual manner protects against danger and angry words.

Marjoram (*Origanum marjorana*)
Mercury.
Mountain Mint, Joy of the Mountain, Wintersweet, Marjorlaine, Knotted Marjorane, Origane.
Marjoram is often used in love spells and potions. Halliwell's "Popular Rhymes and Superstitions" gives the following; *"On St. Luke's Day, says Mother Bunch, take a sprig of Marjoram, Thyme and a little Wormwood; dry them before a fire, rub them to a powder, then sift it through a fine piece of lawn, and simmer it over a slow fire, adding a small quantity of virgin honey and vinegar. Anoint yourself with this when you go to bed, saying the following lines three times, and you will dream of your future partner "that is to be": St. Luke, St. Luke, be kind to me, In dreams let me my true love see."*

The plant is sacred to the goddesses Venus & Aphrodite and can be used in bridal wreaths and marriage decorations to

invoke Her blessing. Strangely, Marjoram is also associated with both Jupiter/Zeus and Thor and, as such, is used in protective spells against thunder and lightening. Grown in the garden it is a general house protective and carrying some in your pocket ensures you will never lack for money. A curious tradition from the West Country of England states that if you bend down to smell it, then it will pull your nose off!

Meadowsweet (*Filipendula ulmaria*)
Jupiter/Venus.
Meadsweet, Dolloff, Queen of the Meadow, Bridewort, Little Queen, Gravel Root, Trumpet Weed.
Well known as a flavouring agent in Mead, Meadowsweet contains more salicylic acid (from which aspirin is synthesized), than Willow bark. Associated in folk-magic with death, its scent was said to induce a sleep from which the victim would never awaken; for this reason it was never placed in sick rooms or bedrooms. Alternatively Meadowsweet is much used in love spells; it can be used dried in poppets and charms, or in incenses and potions. Strewn about the house it brings peace and gladdens the

heart. To find the sex of a thief; gather Meadowsweet at Midsummer and place some on the top of some water in a pottery bowl – if the plant sinks, the thief is a man, if it floats then it is a woman. Associated with goddesses of summer, the blossoms and oils of Meadowsweet can be used to anoint the body or nuptial chamber, prior to going to bed, for that special "Honey Moon" experience.

Melilot (*Melilotus officionalis*)
Sweet Clover, Hart's Tree, Sweet Lucerne, King's Clover, White Melilot, Yellow Melilot.
Melilot, meaning "Honey Lotus", is a great favourite of Bees and produces a beautiful, aromatic honey. The flowers yield a distinctive perfume and a water may also be distilled from the petals, which can be used as a personal scent or magical oil. The whole plant, when dried, can be used either powdered as snuff, or chopped as a tobacco and used as a smoking mixture to relax and calm the nerves prior to ritual. It is used as a preservative or as a binding agent in spells and charms and can be hung up around the house as a protective measure.

Motherwort (*Leonurus cardiaca*)
Venus.
Lion's Tail, Throw Wort.

Motherwort is a strengthening herb. It may be used in incenses or strewn upon an altar in works of magic, to increase the potency of the work. It may be carried in charm bags, in combination with other herbs pertinent to the work, to strengthen and enhance their effect. It is highly protective – being under the influence of the astrological sign Leo – and is a potent ingredient in works of counter-magic. It is considered traditionally to be all-powerful against "wykked sperytis".

Mugwort (*Artemisia vulgaris*)
Venus.
Muggers, Muggons, Felon's Herb, Sailor's Tobacco, Witch Herb, Moderwort, Maiden's Wort.

According to folklore, there is a most potent "coal" concealed at the root of Mugwort, which should be picked on St. Johns Eve and will act as a most effective amulet against all types of venomous serpents and poison. This coal is in fact the dried and acidified remains of old roots, which may be used as an amulet to the same effect. There was a widespread belief that it could give strength and protection, especially to travellers and many would place some in their shoe to this end, some even going so far as to state that it would help a man to walk forty miles before noon, without stopping or becoming tired. Magically speaking, Mugwort has two main uses, one for divination/clairvoyance and the other for protection and banishings. For use in divination it should be made into an infusion (often along with Wormwood), and your crystal, mirror or bowl should be washed in it prior to use. Its juice may be smeared on the back of scrying mirrors to enhance their properties, or the dried or fresh herb placed into the back of the frame. It can be placed under the pillow at night in order to receive prophetic dreams and the tea may be drunk to aid both in remembering dream-work and clairvoyance.

Added together with Wormwood again, it is used as an incense which is burnt during scrying sessions. Mugwort is normally used dried and burnt on charcoal as an incense for banishings, but you can make a kind of "smudge stick" after the Native American manner if you so wish. Collect some stalks of the fresh herb and hang them up to dry for a while until the leaves are limp, but the stalks are still pliable. Next, plait the stalks and leaves together, combining as many as you wish until you have the desired thickness, tying them all in tightly with fine twine as you go. Hang the completed plait back up again out of the Sun until it is dry. Use in the usual way. Mugwort can be used to clear spaces of negative influences, ward off negative or evil spirits or ward off illness and disease. It should be burnt before all major works of exorcism and afterwards to seal the space. As an alternative to an incense, Mugwort may be dried and ground into a powder and either spread around an area or person, or made into sachets or pouches. It tends to have a consistency more wool-like than powder, so is a good binding agent when used with other herbs. It may also be used as a wash or spray, particularly made from a

strong decoction and is traditionally effective for clearing spaces where restless or hostile spirits of the deceased linger, especially at funerals. Hang up in bunches to ward off lightening.

Mullein (*Verbascum thapsus*)
Saturn.
Hag's Taper, Torches, Candlewick, Velvet Dock, Our Lady's Flannel, Aaron's Rod, Rabbit's Ear, Beggar's Blanket, Cuddy's Lungs.
Mullein is primarily a guardian and protective plant. It is said that mediaeval monasteries often grew Mullein plants in their herb gardens to ward against the Devil and there is an ironic symmetry in this. The large stalks of the plant, once dried and dipped in oil or tallow, can be used as "Torches" to light outdoor night time rituals and were often used as such by witches and other magic workers. The leaves, dried and twisted, were also used as lamp wicks in times of need. Mullein can be carried talismanically as a herb of protection and is said to confer courage on the bearer. Sleeping on a pillow stuffed with Mullein will guard against nightmares and hanging bunches of the plant around the room will defend against demons and

evil spirits. As well as conferring protection, the dried leaves may be used in a smoking mixture to gain ancestral knowledge, which is particularly effective around the time of All Hallows. Graveyard Dust, which is called for in some folk charms and spells, can be substituted for dried and finely powdered Mullein herb, if no other is available. Strangely enough, Mullein is also carried to attract the love of the opposite sex.

🌿N🌿

Nettle (*Urtica dioica*)
Mars.
Devil's Plaything, Devil's Leaf, Heg Beg, Hokey Pokey, Stinging Nettle, Jinny Nettle.
Magically speaking, the Nettle is associated with the planet Mars and thus can be used for acts of energy, drive, passion and perhaps revenge. To remove a curse that has been laid against you and return to sender, stuff a poppet with Nettle for a counter magic; keep some in a charm bag about your person as well. Carrying Nettle also wards off ghosts and malefic spirits, whilst dried and sprinkled around the home or your property has the same effect. If you throw a bunch of Nettle

tops onto the fire during a thunderstorm, you will be protected from lightening. Using Nettle as an amulet, worn with a twist of Yarrow, not only allays fear and strengthens courage, but keeps negativity at a far distance. As Nettle is a fiery plant, it has also been used in folk magic to promote lust and in sex magical charms; use in poppets and in charm bags for this purpose or in magical baths.

🌿 P 🌿

Parsley (*Petroselinum crispum*)
Mercury.
Persely, Persele, Devil's Oatmeal, Petersilie, Garden Parsley, Rock Parsley.
Parsley is a contradictory plant, magically speaking. It has associations with ill luck and misfortune, some saying that it is dedicated to the Devil; certainly it must visit Him a certain number of times before it can grow. According to an old Roman belief, Parsley has the power to make a pregnant woman miscarry and eating large quantities was said to procure an abortion. It is unlucky to transplant it from one garden to another, or to give it away and, if you are in love, cutting it will cut your love away. However,

Parsley has been considered to be sacred to St. Peter, Persephone, Venus and Aphrodite, a somewhat strange mixture. To use it magically, it must be cut (!) on a Friday on a waxing Moon. In this case, it may be used as a protective herb, in a purificatory bath before invoking the maternal aspect of any goddess, and in an infusion to gain Ancestral knowledge. Eaten in a deliberately magical manner it can provoke lust and promote fertility, as well as protecting the food on your plate.

Peppermint (*Mentha piperita*)
Mercury.
Brandy Mint, Lammint.
A cooling, calming and healing herb, Peppermint has long been used for these useful properties. It may be used as a visionary herb, being burnt as an incense or taken as a tea, at dusk, to incite dreams of prophecy and divination. Carrying Peppermint is believed to increase prosperity and placing it in one's purse or wallet will attract money to you. The pungent aroma of this herb raises the vibrations of its immediate area; rubbing it on the furniture, walls and floors of you home, or using it in infusion form

as a wash, cleanses all malefic entities from the place and prevents their return. Dried, it can be added to love sachets and poppets and can be drunk as a restorative after long ritual work.

Pennyroyal (*Mentha pulegium*)
Venus.
Pudding Grass, Tickweed, Lurk-in-the-ditch, Run-by-the-Ground, Piliolerial.
This plant is essential used for acts of cleansing and "casting out". Whilst, as a member of the Mint family it is calming and healing, it also has a bit of a fiery undercurrent, so is useful in acts of warding, instead of just sanitising. When worn about the body, it protects against the Evil Eye and gives the advantage in business deals, making sure that you are not swindled. The pulverised herb may be placed under the bed at night to ward against evil spirits and hung about the house for the same purpose. Traditionally it was used to expel fleas, hence one of its folk-names. When used in a charm bag, it may be given to warring couples to bring peace to their relationship and the same charm may be used on board ships to prevent seasickness. Whilst it can be used to calm an

unruly digestion, Pennyroyal is notorious in history for causing illicit abortions, casting out the foetus before its time; therefore this herb should not be used magically by those who are pregnant, or who wish to conceive in the near future. On a brighter note, it is useful in money and wealth spells, combined with honey, or some of your own urine.

Plantain (*Plantago major*)
Venus.

Waybread, Waybroad, Ripple Grass, Englishman's Foot, Broadleaf, Cuckoo's Bread, Rat Tail, Slan-lus.
An ancient, magical plant, to be found in the Anglo-Saxon Nine Herbs Charm, where it is called "Mother of Herbs". Essentially a protective and strengthening plant. In the Anglo-Saxon "Lacnunga", there is the following charm against the "flying venom"; "Take a handful of hammer wort and a handful of maythe (Chamomile) and a handful of Waybroed and roots of water dock, seek those which will float, and one eggshellfull of clean honey, then take clean butter, let him who will help to work up the salve, melt it thrice; let one sing a Mass over the worts, before they are put together and the salve is wrought up." Put a leaf in your

shoe on a long journey and you will not lack
for vitality and be safe from harm. Pluck a
whole plant from the ground and wrap it in
red wool; hang this around your neck or in
any vehicle you are travelling in and you will
be protected against evil spirits as you go.
Carrying a piece of the root in the pocket
protects from snakebites and scorpion
stings, casting out the venom and rendering
it impotent, whilst carrying a piece in your
hatband will prevent and cure headaches. As
the Mother of Herbs, it has especial powers
of protection for and against other women,
when used wisely.

Poppy, Red & White (*Red – Papaver rhoeas;
White – Papaver somniferum*)
Moon.
*Common Poppy, Corn Poppy, Field Poppy,
Thundercup, Thunderflower, Lightnings, Corn
Rose, Mawseed.*
This plant has symbolised both fertility and
death for thousands of years, wherever it
has been found. It is associated with both
the female Powers of the crops, growth,
ripeness and harvest and also with the Spirit
of the dying male Powers that are sacrificed
in autumn. The milky-white juice that comes

from the stem and head when they are cut symbolises the milk of a lactating mother and the blood-red petals are associated with the death of the year's crops as they graphically fall to the ground. In magical practice, it is mostly the seeds or seed heads that are used. Carrying the dried seeds is said to promote fertility and attract good fortune and prosperity and to become pregnant, the seeds should be added to all food that is eaten. The dried seed heads may be emptied of their contents and used as the receptacles for spells; the request should be written on a small piece of paper and inserted into the seed head and placed under the pillow at night. The Powers should be invoked to bring about the desired end and, if you dream of the spell in the night, then your work will be successful. Traditionally, the dried seed heads were often gilded and worn as talismans to attract wealth. To make yourself invisible, Poppy seeds should be soaked in wine for 15 days. The wine should then be drunk, once a day for 5 days, whilst fasting. At the end of this period, you will have the ability to make yourself invisible at will. Poppy has also been used for visionary purposes; the safest way is to use the seeds in an incense whilst scrying

or divining, or to smoke the bedroom prior to sleep, which will produce prophetic dreams. The whole plant may be placed in the rafters or house timbers, to keep lightening away from the home. It is traditional to bake the seeds into small honey cakes and leave these out as offerings to the Ancestors and the Spirits of the Dead.

Privet (*Ligustrum vulgare*)
Moon.
Zaunriegel.
The berries and leaves of this small tree are mildly toxic and can cause allergic reactions if swallowed, so internal use is to be avoided. Generally a protective and defensive plant, but little known or used magically. The wood may be carved into small protective fetishes that may be carried on the person, or the bark burnt as a protective incense. The Privet is usually used as a hedging plant, which, when placed with magical intent, can ward your property from unwanted, outside influences. Alternatively, small lengths of the wood may be carved with protective charms/sigils, and strung together on a line; these can then be tied up as a magical barrier to prevent unwanted intrusions of all kinds.

95

❧R❧

Rosemary (*Rosmarinus officionalis*)
Sun.
Dew-of-the-Sea, Rosa Maria, Compass-weed, Incensier, Polar Plant, Romarin, Elf-Leaf, Guardrobe.

This is an especially potent plant, lending strength to searches into the past and beyond the veil and having also a wide range of uses. "Rosemary for remembrance" is a well-known adage and harks back to the Roman custom of placing bunches of Rosemary in the coffin at funerals and it would be planted around tombs later on. During the Mediaeval period in England it was used as an antidote to the Black Death and so its association with death and remembrance has a long history. In some forms of Craft Rosemary is one of the plants woven into a wreath that

is used to garland the Stang, representing the Lord of Death, at the Hallowmas rites. Its strong and pungent smell is a distinctive addition to incense at this time of year and it may also be used in rites of divination for the clarity of thought it brings. It is sometimes baked into cakes to be eaten during the Hallowmas observances and is hung up around the ritual area in honour and remembrance of the Ancestors at this time. It is also dedicated to the Virgin Mary in Christian tradition and was used as a ward against witches and evil spirits hung up in the home, and against the Night Mare when placed under pillows. Its strong and fragrant smell makes it exceedingly attractive in any warding or protective actions and it has been used for centuries in this manner, retaining its scent long after the leaves have dried out. Hung up on the doorpost it deters thieves from entering the house and carrying a bunch keeps you healthy. It has also long been used in love and lust magic, being used to stuff poppets and sachets with this intent. It is particularly attractive to the Elven kind and burning Rosemary as an incense will attract their close attention. The mediaeval "Stockholm Herbal" manuscript states that

if a man or woman bears a staff or stalk of this plant then, "it kepyth hym fro thresse" (malicious or dangerous supernatural beings).

Rue (*Ruta graveolens*)
Sun/Mars.
Herb of Grace, Herbygrass, Ruta, Rewe, Hreow.
Long used as a protection against witches and malefic magic, Rue is used as a powerful expellant herb. It is one of the ingredients in the traditional Thieves Vinegar mixture, used to cleanse and guard against detection, disease and negativity on all levels. A strong charm to protect the home and all within uses Rue; take a good sprig of the herb, a morsel of bread, some ash from the hearth and something personal from each member of the house. Tie all these into a small bundle and secrete somewhere about the house. Alternatively, a dried sprig of Rue may be employed as the famed Cimaruta charm, either by itself or with other charms attached with red thread. Rue is greatly employed as a herb in exorcisms, either as an incense or a wash and is beneficial in charms for countermagic. Like all herbs of this nature though, Rue may also be employed in acts of malefic magic itself

and the expression, "You will rue the day..." comes from the belief that this was a plant of misfortune. To bring disaster on a marriage, wait until the couple emerge from the church, throw a large sprig of Rue to the ground before them and say; "I cast Rue before you and on all you do." Strangely, Rue is also known as a herb that is useful in acts of astral projection and visionary work, being able to carry you out into the realms of the Otherworld; take as a tea or use as an incense. (Use Rue with caution; it contains toxins that many are allergic to and should not be used during pregnancy).

𝕊

Sage (*Salvia officionalis*)
Jupiter.
Sawge, Garden Sage, Red Sage, Salvia salvatrix.
Sage is traditionally grown in the garden alongside Rue, so that it may be protected and its energies be kept pure. Long held as a sacred and health-giving herb, it must be collected only under ritual conditions; first you must take a bath and ritually cleanse yourself, then dress in a white robe and, going barefoot, gather the plant without

using an iron knife. Sage is used in incenses to cleanse and clear a place, person or atmosphere. As a tea, it may be taken to ritually cleanse before any work of magic and to strengthen the constitution for the work. It was used in love divinations and as a memorial to the dead in many country districts and gave rise to the old rhyme; "He that would live for aye, Must eat Sage in May." Carrying the plant grants wisdom to the bearer and protects from the evil eye. It is used in healing and prosperity spells and placing it under your pillow at night promotes prophetic dreams. If these are of bad fortune, bury the leaves immediately upon waking and you will avert the the ill luck.

Sanicle (*Sanicula europaea*)
Mars.
Wood Sanicle, Poolroot, Self-Heal.
Sanicle has a great reputation as a healing herb, mostly for wounds and for blood disorders. Healing poppets and charm bags will benefit from being stuffed with this herb and it should be employed in incenses, spells and petitions to that end. So powerful was this plant thought to be that

in the Middle Ages it gave rise to the saying;
"He that hath Sanicle, hath no need of a
surgeon." The wise witch would do well to
heed this advice.

Savory (*Satureia hortensis*)
Mercury.
Summer Savory, Garden Savory.
Savory has been cultivated for thousands
of years and was used before spices were
imported from the East Indies; it was used
by the Romans to add flavour to their dishes
and to bring joy and good times to feasts. It
was supposed to belong to the lusty wood
spirits, the Satyrs, hence the Latin name of
the genus, and was used frequently as an
aphrodisiac. As a magical herb, it may be
used in culinary magics to bring good spirits
to a meal and increase the sense of mirth
and it is also reputed to strengthen the mind
and spirit when carried or worn.

Shepherd's Purse (*Capsella bursa-pastoris*)
Mercury.
*Shepherd's Bag, Lady's Purse, Witches Pouches,
Case-weed, Sanguinary, Mother's Heart, Shovelweed,
Toywort, Clappedepouch.*
The botanical name means "the little case

of the shepherd", which refers to the small, triangular seed-cases which resemble the purses once commonly worn by old-time shepherds on their belts. The Irish name of "Clappedepouch" refers to the begging of Lepers, who stood at crossroads with a bell or clapper, receiving alms in a cup at the end of a long pole. Magically, Shepherds Purse was used as a protective charm against bleeding. The seeds were used as an amulet for teething children. Eating the seeds of the first three Shepherd's Purse plants one sees is said to protect against all manner of diseases for the rest of the year.

Skullcap (*Scutellaria galericulata*)
Saturn.
Common Scullcap, Greater Scullcap, Helmet Flower, Hoodwort, Mad-dog, Madweed.
The common name of "Skullcap" refers either to the shape of the tiny flowers, which resemble the cap worn by a Cardinal (hence also Helmet Flower), or to the fact that it was frequently prescribed for mental conditions. It is used magically as a "binding" plant, in that it is used to seal promises and oaths and promote fidelity between partners. It may be used

at weddings and handfastings to unite a loving couple, either as an incense, or in the Loving Cup presented to them to drink from. However, beware that should the promise or oath be broken, the plant will exact a severe penalty on the oath-breaker. A wife may wear Skullcap as a charm about her person, to protect her husband against the charms and advances of other women.

Southernwood (*Artemisia abrotanum*)
Mercury.
Lad's Love, Old Man, Boy's Love, Maid's Ruin, Appleringie.
This is the southern European equivalent to

the more northerly Wormwood and a member of the same family of aromatic herbs. Its strong scent was considered to be highly aphrodisiac at one time and used to be presented by young men to the ladies of their

choice. Therefore it is a good plant to use in love spells of all kinds. It can be placed in the bedroom and also under the bed to arouse lustful thoughts. Conversely, also because of it's sharp aroma, it is thought to be a very protective plant. Use it to ward off all forms of "infection", such as malignant entities and malefic spells. In an incense, it can sharpen the mind, ward off drowsiness and focus the mind on the work at hand.

Spearmint (*Mentha spicata*)
Venus.
Spire Mint, Our Lady's Mint, Garden Mint, Green Mint, Lamb Mint, Mackerel Mint.
A gentler and more softly scented version of Peppermint, this herb is generally used for very similar purposes. It is particularly useful in spells for healing stubborn lung conditions and, for protection during the night, stuff a herb pillow and sleep with it beneath your head. It is a more welcoming herb than its compatriot and hence is of more use in incenses intended to greet and thank the spirits that you are used to working with. Use as an offering to the Faere Folk and to the plants that you work with in the wild.

St. Johnswort (*Hypericum perforatum*)
Sun.

Hypericum, Faerie Herb, Fuga Daemonum, Goat Weed, Amber.

This herb has been known as a highly magical plant for hundreds of years, due to its protective and defensive powers against negative forces. Known as "Fuga Daemonum" – Flight of Demons – during the mediaeval period, it was used by herbalists as a smoke to banish foul airs and disease. In the old rhyme; "St John's Wort, Vervain, Trefoil, Dill, Hinder Witches of their will," it is combined with other well known "banishing" herbs to create a charm or incense against malefic attacks. Banckes' Sixteenth-century Herball says that, "If it be putte in a Mannes house there shall come no wycked sprite therein." It is considered most beneficial to wear a protective sprig when going to war and both men and women have used it to attract the attention of the opposite sex. It is most effective when picked on Midsummer's Eve, still wet with dew. If a maiden gathers it, fasting, she will be wed within the year; if she places the herb under her pillow, she will see his face beforehand. If a woman is barren and she

picks the herb at this time, naked, then she will conceive and bear a child before next Midsummer. The herb also has the power to deflect or counteract the ill effects of Faerie magic – hence one of its common names. Its protective powers are considered to be strengthened by the fact that it "weeps" a blood red juice when it is "ripe". The herb would be added to the Midsummer fires – along with other herbs – for the smoke to billow across the land and protect the ripening crops in the fields from disease and evil intent. Take a large sprig of the herb – collected at Midsummer – and place it in a glass jar and stopper it tightly; hang this in the main window of your home and it will protect against thunderbolts, fire and malefic spirits.

❦T❧

Tansy (*Tanacetum vulgare*)
Venus.
Buttons, Bitter Buttons, Wormwort, Parsley Fern, English Cost, Stinking Willie.
Tansy is known for its preservative and protective properties and its magical uses reflect this. It was used as a strewing

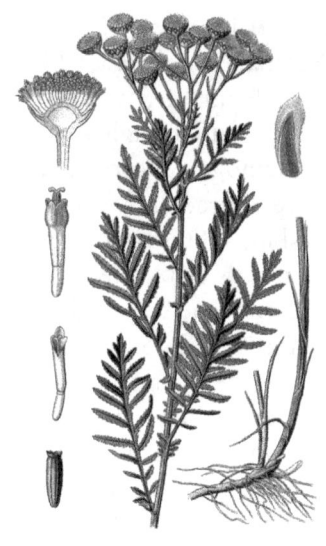

herb, to preserve corpses and added to cakes during Lent to remind folk of the bitter herbs eaten at the original Passover. Magically it can be used in spells and charms to preserve and lengthen life, traditionally being placed in shoes to cure stubborn fevers. An incense containing Tansy may be used to clear an area of noxious energies and to preserve its atmosphere for ritual or sacred purposes. Cakes may be made at the time of the Vernal Equinox for ritual use, containing Tansy; these will reflect the time of renewal and regeneration.

Thorn Apple (*Datura stramonium*)
Jupiter.
Datura, Jimson-weed, Devil's Apple, Ghost Flower, Mad apple, Mad Weed, Angel's Trumpet, Witches Thimble.

107

Thorn apple is a herb to be wary of. As a member of the Solanaceae family, like Deadly Nightshade and Henbane, it can be highly toxic if ingested, even though it has been used for its hallucinogenic properties for centuries. Its active ingredients can be absorbed through the skin, so it is best to use gloves when handling it in its raw state. Used externally it is a valuable spell ingredient when dried and powdered. It can be sprinkled around an area that has been "overlooked" to break the spell or curse, and will ward against further negative intrusions. In an incense it is useful to induce astral projection/spirit travelling, but this is best done out of doors. The priests of Apollo in ancient Greece used its smoke to prophecy and it has also been used as an aphrodisiac with mixed results. This plant is also employed in binding love spells; use the dried pod, emptied of seeds, and add objects from your loved one. Enchant this whilst bound with black thread and they will surely come to you.

(Interestingly, there is another object that is also called a "Thorn Apple", that has nothing to do with Datura. This is an actual Apple, which has been studded with 12 thorns or pins. It is then used by those

that have "the gift" as a summoning charm and is exceedingly effective).

Thyme (*Thymus vulgaris*)
Venus.
Common Thyme, Garden Thyme, Mother Thyme, Running Thyme, Shepherd's Thyme.
Thyme was used by the ancient Greeks as a fumigatory herb (from whence it derives its name), and as cleanser prior to all rituals; this is still good practice today and it should be used as an incense to smoke any area before magical work. Thyme protects against all dangerous spirits, creatures, insects and animals. It strengthens the spirit and increases courage in those that bear it and is also said to bestow the ability to see the Faere Folk when carried. Thyme has long been considered as a funereal herb and is used to re-establish contact with the ancestors and recently departed family members. It may be carried, used as an incense or taken internally in infusion form, the departed spirits then being summoned to ask advice of them, or to send them messages and blessings. The souls of the dead take refuge in Thyme; when someone dies, Thyme may be taken into the house and kept there until the body is taken

for burial, then cast into the grave. Wearing a sprig of Thyme in your clothing, or casting one into the fire with intent, is said to attract good fortune and health and a woman may wear a sprig in her hair if she wishes to become irresistible to the opposite sex. In the Spring of the year, taking a magical bath composed of sprigs of Thyme and Marjoram, will ensure all sorrows and ills are removed and clears the way for a beneficial year ahead.

Tormentil (*Potentilla tormentilla*)
Sun.
Septfoil, Thormantle, Biscuits, Bloodroot, Earthbank, Ewe Daisy, Flesh and Blood, Shepherd's Knot.
Whilst an infusion of this herb may be given to a loved one to keep their love and affection, the main use of this plant is protective. The same infusion may be taken by oneself for general protection and Spiritualist Mediums are known to drink this, as a guard against being permanently possessed by their Spirit Guides and other Spirits. Bunches or sprigs of the herb may be hung up in the home to protect against fire and lightening and to drive away malignant spirits, hence one of it's folk names – Thormantle.

V

Valerian (*Valeriana officionalis*)
Mercury.
*Phu, St. George's Herb, All-Heal, Amantilla,
Setwall, Setewale, Capon's Tail, Vandal Root,
Herb of Witches, Bloody Butcher, Pretty Betsy.*
As a herb of protection, Valerian can
be hung in the home to protect against
lightening, evil spirits and to stop warring
couples from fighting. This herb attracts
rats and it has been suggested that it was the

111

"secret weapon" that was used by the Pied Piper of Hamlin to rid the city of its plague. When working with the rat as a spirit animal, Valerian may be used as an attractant and a reward for work done. The herb is reputed to have aphrodisiac qualities and a young woman who carried this herb about her was said never to lack for ardent lovers. Use also in love charms and sachets. Witches have used Valerian for many centuries to help bond with cats, either as physical familiars or with their spirit equivalent. As some forms of the Faere Folk are said to enjoy taking on feline form, Valerian may also be used to encourage and attract these types to come and work with you.

Violet (*Viola riviniana*)
Venus.
Common Dog-Violet, Dog Violet, Wood Violet.
Most magical traditions concerning Violets refer to the Sweet Violet (Viola odorata), and revolve around the scent of that plant and its uses. The Dog Violet is so-named as it has no discernible scent and, hence, is not used for the same purposes. The only uses I have been able to uncover for this variant is in liminal sleep or dream

travelling. The time between sleep and waking is sometimes known as "Violet Time", so place a sachet or charm bag of fresh Violets under your pillow, with the intention of going on a journey. Use the power of this plant to achieve separation from your body and to direct you to the Other-realms, where you may seek for magical help and guidance of all kinds. As this plant is also found growing mostly in woodland and forested areas, use it for anything to do with Green Magic and in contacting the Spirits of those areas.

Vervain (*Verbena officionalis*)
Venus.
Herb of Grace, Enchanters Herb, Herba Veneris, Juno's Tears, Holy Herb, Van Van, Pigeon Grass, Devil's Hate, Brittanica.
Vervain has been used for both magical and medicinal purposes for millennia. A favourite of the Druids, they used it in an infusion to wash their altars prior to making sacrifices. The Romans used it to scatter on their altars to sanctify them and dedicated the plant to Venus. It was one of the prime herbs of Anglo-Saxon times, being much favoured by clergy and common folk alike for all kinds of ills and

113

ailments. In particular it was used in their Holy Salve and the Elizabethans were addicted to its use in love potions and philtres, for which it is ideally suited, being dedicated to Venus. All parts of the plant are used and traditionally it must be picked at the rising of the Dog Star, Sirius, when the light of neither Sun nor Moon is in the sky. It must be plucked with the left hand only and a libation of honey must be left in its place to appease the Earth Wights. It is a plant very well disposed towards people and will do its best to aid them, if treated with respect and consideration. Magically it is used mainly as a protective charm and for cleansing a place or person. It can be made into a strong infusion by steeping in wine or spirits, which is then used as a wash or sprinkled around a place or person. Warriors would keep a piece about them when going into battle, either sewn into their clothes or worn in a bag and sorcerers would bind a piece round their brows' during ritual to protect from demons. It was hung up in the house to protect against evil spirits, either tied up in bundles, bags or poppets and these are a good defence especially against predatory or parasitic entities. It is a protection against black magic and wards off bad dreams if hung around the neck and will

aid in casting a glamour to hide from enemies, especially when prepared as an ointment. It may be used to reverse negative spells and is of use in exorcisms. It has also been used as a safer form of herb in "Flying Ointments"; infuse the herb in oil and add beeswax and other herbs to your desired end.

🎕W🎕

Wild Strawberry (*Fragraria vesca*)
Venus.
Wood Strawberry, Woodland Strawberry, Woodman's Delight.
Deriving from the now obsolete term "straw" from the verb "to strew", the name of the Wild Strawberry refers to its habit of sending out a tangle of vines to cover the ground around itself. This much smaller cousin of the modern cultivated varieties have long been used in love magic in various ways. The leaves may be carried for luck in love and the fruit served as an aphrodisiac, or to attract the attention of your loved one. The beautiful scent of the ripe fruit can be captured in a wine that is used for handfastings and/or as a loving cup. This wine may also be used at Midsummer, either

as a libation to the Faere Folk, or to facilitate contact with them, if they are willing. The dried fruit and leaves may be included in sachets and poppets designed to bring two people together in a loving union and the leaves may be included in an incense for the same purpose. Carrying a small packet of Wild Strawberry seeds and leaves is a traditional charm to ease the pains of labour for pregnant women.

Witch Hazel (*Hamamelis virginiana*)
Sun.
Spotted Alder, Winterbloom, Snapping Hazelnut.
The twigs of Witch Hazel have long been used as divining rods, hence the common name of this plant. The usage was first known to the peoples of North America and the knowledge was passed back to Europe by incoming magic-workers. The twigs and stripped bark of this plant are used to protect against evil influence and malefic spells, either in incenses, charm bags, or twined together to form protective poppets. The astringent nature of this useful plant make it an ideal herb for cleansing and protective purposes and

washes and sprays can be made from it for these purposes, using magical intent. It is said that if you have a broken heart, then carrying Witch Hazel can help to heal it and it will also aid in cooling fiery passions.

Woodruff (*Galium odoratum*)
Mars.
Sweet Woodruff, Wuderove, Wood-rova, Master of the Woods, Star Grass, Herb Walter, Waldmeister's Tea.
The fresh plant has little scent, but when dried gives rise to the name of "Sweet". Long used for its scent in clearing atmospheres and homes of negative and "dirty" energies, it is renowned for being added to wine. This is the herb that is infused in various wines to create a specially flavoured wine in May for welcoming in the Summer months. It is often used ritually for this purpose and lasts well throughout the Summer. Bunches of the plant were used in Christian magic, hung up in churches and cathedrals as protective charms against evil. Carrying Sweet Woodruff is said to attract victory – particularly for athletes and warriors – and will bring you money and prosperity. Carrying Woodruff tied

up in a soft, leather pouch is a traditional charm to protect against all harm. The dried and finely powdered herb may be scattered around any ritual area to purify it and lend its fragrance to any ritual performed there. The powder may also be used as an addition to incenses, as it acts as a fixative for other scents, similarly to Orris Root.

Wormwood (*Artemisia absinthium*)
Mars.
Absinthe, Old Woman, King's Crown.
Very similar in usage to Mugwort, to which it is a close cousin, Wormwood is much stronger and should not be taken internally in large doses, as it can cause hallucinations and even brain damage. Despite this – and probably for this very reason – Wormwood has long been used for scrying, to aid in divinations and for contacting Spirits. The juice may be smeared onto a variety of tools for seeing into the Otherworlds, dried and used in incenses and carried about the person in bunches for the same purpose. This is particularly effective if done in old graveyards, as the Spirits are said to

be attracted to this particular plant and will come at your call if you use it there. Wormwood can also be used as a strong cleansing and banishing herb and is of great use when counteracting charms of malefic bewitchment. It also protects against the bites of Sea Dragons.

$$\maltese Y \maltese$$

Yarrow (*Achillea millefolium*)
Venus.
Milfoil, Woundwort, Carpenter's Weed, Devil's Plaything, Devil's Nettle, Old Man's Pepper, Bloodwort, Yarroway, Sneezewort.
Yarrow is one of the herbs that are traditionally associated with the Old Horned One and most often used, magically, in divinations, particularly love charms. There are many of these and here are but two. A young woman should sew up an ounce of Yarrow herb into a flannel sachet and, placing it under her pillow at night, should say; "Thou pretty herb of Venus' tree, Thy true name is Yarrow; Now who my true bosom friend must be, Pray tell thou me tomorrow." She must then go to sleep and would

dream of her future lover/husband that very night. The Yarrow for this charm must be picked from a graveyard on the night of the Full Moon. Another charm from the Eastern counties uses a serrated leaf of Yarroway. The inside of the nose is tickled with the leaf, whilst the following lines are spoken; "Yarroway, Yarroway, bear a white blow; If my love love me, my nose will bleed now." If the operation causes the nose to bleed, then it is a certain sign of success. Yarrow is also used to exorcise negativity and evil from places; when worn it protects the wearer from all ill and bestows great courage and banishes all fear. Bunches of the herb may be hung above the cradles of new-born babies to protect them from ill-wishing and it was also a sign that there was a magic-worker about. As the old saying goes; "Where Yarrow grows, there is one who Knows."

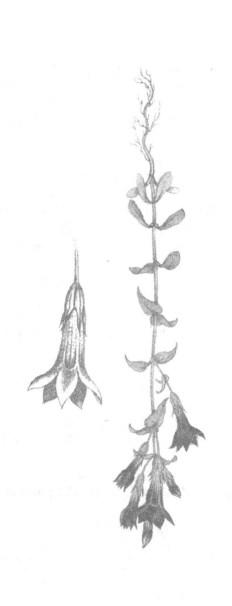

Selected Bibliography and Suggested Reading List

Andrews, Steve. *Herbs of the Northern Shaman.* O Books 2010. ISBN 978-1-84694-369-0.

Bartram, Thomas. *Bartram's Encyclopaedia of Herbal Medicine.* Constable & Robinson Ltd. 1998. ISBN 1-85487-586-8.

Beyerl, Paul. *The Master Book of Herbalism.* Phoenix Publishing Co. 1996. ISBN 0-919345-53-0.

Boyer, Corinne. *Under the Witching Tree.* Troy Books 2017. ISBN 978-1-909602-18-2.

Bruton-Seal, Julie. *Hedgerow Medicine; Harvest and Make your own Herbal Remedies.* Merlin Unwin Books 2008. ISBN 978-1873674994.

Conway, David. *The Magic of Herbs.* Mayflower Books Ltd. 1977. ISBN 583-12427-5.

Culpepper, Nicholas. *Culpepper's Complete Herbal.* Foulsham Press. N.D.

Davies, Marion. *The Magical Lore of Herbs.* Capall Bann 1994. ISBN 1-898307-14-8.

Duffy, Martin. *Effigy; Of Graven Image and Holy Idol.* Three Hands Press 2015.

Gary, Gemma. *The Black Toad; West Country Witchcraft and Magic.* Troy Books 2012. ISBN 978- 0-9561043-7-3.

Gary, Gemma. *Traditional Witchcraft: A Cornish Book of Ways.* Troy Books 2015. ISBN 978-0- 9561043-4-2.

Grieve, Mrs M. *A Modern Herbal.* Tiger Books International PLC 1998. ISBN 1-85501-249-9.

Harleian Ms. *Lacnunga – Liber medicinalis de virtutibus herbarum.* British Museum.

Hatfield, Gabrielle. *Country Remedies; Traditional East Anglian Plant Remedies in the 21st Century.* The Boydell Press 2002. ISBN 0-85115-563-4.

Hatsis, Thomas. *The Witches' Ointment; The Secret History of Psychedelic Magic.* Park Street Press 2017.ISBN 978-1-62055-473-9.

Howard, Michael. *A-Z of Traditional Herbal Remedies.* Senate Press Ltd. 1997. ISBN 1-85958-504- 4.

Huson, Paul. *Mastering Herbalism.* Madison Books 2001. ISBN 1-56833-181-9.

Hyslop, Jon & Ratcliffe, Paul. *A Folk Herbal.* Radiation Publications 1989. ISBN 1-871889-00-6.

Jacob, Dorothy. *A Witch's Guide to Gardening.* Elek Books Ltd. 1964.

King, Graham. *The British Book of Spells and Charms.* Troy Books 2016. ISBN 978-1-909602-17-   5.

Lavender, Susan & Franklin, Anna. *Herb Craft; A Guide to the Shamanic & Ritual Use of Herbs.* Capall Bann 1996. ISBN 1-898307-57-9.

Muller-Ebeling,   Claudia.   Ratsch, Christian. & Storl, Wolf-Dieter. *Witchcraft Medicine; Healing Arts, Shamanic Practice & Forbidden Plants.* Inner Traditions 2003. ISBN 0-89281-971-5.

Pollington, Stephen. *Leechcraft; Early English Charms, Plantlore & Healing.* Anglo-Saxon Books   2011. ISBN 9781898281474.

Pearson, Nigel G. *The Devil's Plantation; East Anglian Lore, Witchcraft & Folk-Magic.* Troy Books 2016. ISBN 9-781909-602113.

Pearson, Nigel G. *Treading the Mill; Workings in Traditional Witchcraft.* Troy Books 2017. ISBN   978-1-909602-21-2.

Pearson, Nigel G. *Walking the Tides; Seasonal Magical Rhythms and Lore.* Troy Books 2017. ISBN   978-1-909602-27-4.

Rohde, Eleanour Sinclair. *Herbs and Herb Gardening.* The Medici Society 1945.

Roth, Harold. *The Witching Herbs; 13 Essential Plants and Herbs for your Magical Garden.* Weiser Books 2017. ISBN 978-1-57863-599-3.

Schulke, Daniel A. *Viridarium Umbris; The Pleasure Garden of Shadow.* Xoanon Publishing 2005.